A MIND PRETENDING TO BE ME

*How A F*cked-Up Mind
Can Set You Free*

KATHERINE KEEN VELASQUEZ

© 2026 Katherine Keen Velasquez

ISBN: 979-8-9934759-6-7

Imprint: Independently published

All rights reserved.

No part of this book may be reproduced in any form without written permission from the author.

Cover artwork by Ferdinando Fusco

Cover and interior design by Simona Esposito

Edited by Lia Ottaviano

The author is not engaged in rendering professional advice or services to the individual reader. The ideas, procedures, and suggestions contained in this book are not intended as a substitute for consulting with your physician. All matters regarding your health require medical supervision. The author shall not be liable or responsible for any loss or damage allegedly arising from any information or suggestion in this book.

For my husband, who never ceases to inspire me and who I adore. And for my daughters, who are completely perfect.

I love you with all my heart.

TABLE OF CONTENTS

ACKNOWLEDGMENTS	9
INTRODUCTION	11
HOW TO READ THIS BOOK	14
KEY TERMS TO HELP YOU UNDERSTAND THIS BOOK	16
PART 1: THE PROBLEM – HOW WE GET LOST IN THE MIND	**18**
What Is a Fucked-Up Mind	19
My Story	23
The Birth of the Self-Image	42
PART 2: THE MIND – WHAT IT IS AND WHAT IT ISN'T	**46**
You Are Not Your Fucked-Up Mind	47
Your Thoughts Are Not True	52
The Human Superpower	58
PART 3: THE SELF IMAGE – A CREATIVE MASTERPIECE SO GOOD IT FOOLED YOU	**60**
The Wild Creation of Intrusive Thoughts	61
You Are Not Who You Think You Are	68
The Mind Does Not Control What You Do	77

PART 4: THE ONE TRUTH – THE INTELLIGENCE AND LOVE THAT YOU ARE   79

    All the Voices That Are Not You   80
    Fall in Love With the Love Story of Your Life   94
    Your Problem Doesn't Exist   99
    Your Mind Will Never Find the Answer to the Problem   112

PART 5: THE ONE UNIVERSAL ADDICTION   122

    A Critical Missing Link   123
    The Original Addiction   128
    Exchanging Magic for Myth   138

PART 6: A MISUSED MIND – HOW IT KEEPS YOU SMALL   141

    A Wasted Superpower   142
    The Tail Chase of Futility   145
    When It Pays to Be Miserable   152
    Turning Away from the True Identity   158

PART 7: AN UNLIKELY GUIDE – LET THE FUCKED-UP MIND SHOW YOU THE MAGIC OF WHO YOU ARE   160

    Healing by Seeing   161
    Trust the Lover That Moves You   172
    Don't Live in the Past   182
    Where Is Your Energy Going?   197
    Afraid of Myself   203
    The Nightmare That Wakes You Up   212

PART 8: WAKING UP   **224**
    Build the Muscle of Being With Discomfort   225
    Love Your Fucked-Up Mind   228
    The Mind Saves You, But Not How You Think   231
    Practices to Promote Freedom   237

CONCLUSION   **241**

REFERENCE LIST   **244**

ACKNOWLEDGMENTS

I wanted thank my husband for all the ways he has loved me, supported me, and believed in me. Without him, this book would not exist.

There are many people who have taught me and held a candle for me along my path. The two that I could not go without mentioning are Clare Dimond and Marnix Pauwels. I will forever be grateful to them for their work and teaching.

I wanted to thank my parents for never giving up and for giving me a great deal of love and care.

Finally, I wanted to thank my very generous beta readers, Ferdinando Fusco, Grace Keen, and Tito Velasquez.

INTRODUCTION

This is a love story. It is a love story that likely every human being has participated in, in addition to any other thrilling or lackluster romances they might have had. It is the story of how you and I have become enamored and fallen in love with the mind. It had to happen, really. We enter this world as innocent children who have no use for the mind other than imagining fairies and dragons and endless games. Then we encounter bigger obstacles and people who tell us that what we do is wrong and not enough. And the mind is the perfect security blanket to fall into—an ever-present protector always whispering in our ear, willing to analyze, justify, and strategize on our behalf. So we fall in love with the mind. We get lost in the mind. We mistakenly believe that the voice in our mind is our voice. Plenty of people live their whole lives that way. For some, this subconscious romance and enmeshment with the mind yields a fine life. For others, like myself, the mind in this misguided role creates a whole world of problems that lead to severe mental messes commonly labeled as anxiety, depression, and OCD (to name a few). Thankfully, in my version of this story, life handed me a twist in the form of a near-mental breakdown that disrupted the very mediocre stability that I was experiencing in my love story. That twist felt as if it would break me, but it delivered me into a whole new life of greater understanding, love, and peace.

I wrote this book because I would like to be part of the twist in your love story with the mind. Mental illness of any kind can often seem so fixed, so consuming, so permanent. But when you begin to wake up to your enamored trance with the mind and the confusion it has caused about your true identity, anything can shift and change, and anything is possible. In short, mental illness is an invitation, a doorway, to spiritual awakening.

Also, let me be clear. In no way am I attempting to convince you that your mind is bad or useless. The mind is, in fact, our greatest superpower when it is used for what it was intended. However, when the mind is put in the position of an authoritative guide, all hell breaks loose.

So this book is for anyone who has experienced mental illness of any kind. You will see many examples of anxiety disorder and OCD intrusive thoughts because those are the struggles I have experienced the most. But if you have experienced mental illness of any kind, you will benefit from what I share. Here's to seeing through illusions and waking up to what is true. Who knows where it will lead us?

HOW TO READ THIS BOOK

This book is my love letter to you. It is an outpouring from my heart to yours based on all my experiences and everything I have learned up to this point. In it, you will not find homework and to-do lists. From my experience, healing and shifts in awareness often do not come from those things. You will find an expression of the truth through my lens. We all live in different worlds, worlds that are created by the lens of our experiences, what we have learned, and what we believe. However, we all have the opportunity to uncover and remember the love and intelligence that we truly are when everything else is stripped away. This book is my version of that truth and the largely raw and unfiltered story of how I found it. When we are exposed to this one truth, it can touch the intelligence of our being and shine light on confusion and misunderstanding. This happens because the love and intelligence that is your identity can recognize itself in anyone else's story. When it recognizes itself, it lights up with a deep resonance, and its signal grows stronger. This is how healing happens. This is how pain falls away, how lifelong burdens are lifted, how untrue stories are seen through, and how behavior changes.

So, as you read this love letter that was written for you, don't worry about what your mind has to say. This love letter was not written to your mind. It was written to the essence of your being, to the intelligence and love that you are. Don't pay attention to what you think. Instead, pay attention to how you feel. If you feel any sense of lightness, hope, or freedom, then you are on the right track. And if someone else gives you this feeling, then put this book down and read or listen to them instead.

My love letter is from the intelligence of my being to the intelligence of yours. With great irony, the most appropriate words that I can think of to launch us into this book are from the wildly misinterpreted Bible, "And you will know (recognize) the truth, and the truth will set you free." In that spirit, here we go.

KEY TERMS TO HELP YOU UNDERSTAND THIS BOOK

- The Mind: The space where thoughts appear. This term is interchangeable with "the imagination." The thoughts that cross this space can include ideas, seemingly divine inspiration, as well as the narrating "I" (see next key term).
- The Narrating "I": When I talk about this, I am referring to thoughts that appear in your mind that are spoken in first person (e.g., I feel…, I want…, I hate…, etc.) in a voice that you associate with your own. This is your personal narrator.
- The Ego: I use this term to describe the self-image that we carry that began forming when we were children. It is the idea of ourselves that holds all of our deepest fears and insecurities that we think we need to protect. It is also the source of the narrating "I" (see previous term).

- Intelligence: I use this term to describe your true self or your true nature and the force that is animating your body (and everyone else's).

PART 1:
THE PROBLEM – HOW WE GET LOST IN THE MIND

CHAPTER 1
WHAT IS A FUCKED-UP MIND?

This is a book for people who have fucked-up minds. Even more, this is a book for people who have fucked-up minds and who have tried everything within their reach to fix it. Your gender, race, age, and ethnicity are completely irrelevant. If you have experienced any form of mental illness, then this book is for you. Having a fucked-up mind can mean any number of things, but it boils down to having any mental or emotional experience that your mind says shouldn't be there or should be different. You might experience things like depression, anxiety, intrusive thoughts, OCD, postpartum anxiety or depression, rage, jealousy, obsessions, compulsions… You get the idea. I'm talking about having repetitive thoughts, feelings, and accompanying bodily sensations that feel like they haunt you or damage your quality of life. What I say applies to every single kind of mental illness, and you will benefit regardless of what version plays out in your mind.

I have a fucked-up mind. It blabbers on incessantly. It argues with itself. It creates problems and then works hard to solve them. It worries incessantly. It often sounds dark and hopeless. It paints horrific images of my demise and the demise of those that I love. It spits out images of me doing things that I would never ever want to do…over and over again. And with many of these productions, my body goes into a frozen panic. While all of this is true (albeit far less frequent), I am experiencing sanity like I never have before. I have a fucked-up mind AND for the first time in my life, I am sane. It sounds ridiculous, right? But I promise that it's true. The amazing thing is that the content of your mind has absolutely nothing to do with your sanity. The belief in the content of your mind, on the other hand, has everything to do with your sanity. That might sound completely nonsensical right now, but don't worry. That's what this book is for.

We live in a culture that is obsessed with our mental state and doing things to fix it. We go to unimaginable lengths to accomplish this. We talk about the past, we numb ourselves with pills, we drink, we do drugs, we hypnotize ourselves, we get acupuncture, we do energy work, we dunk our bodies in freezing water or walk on burning coals. Many of these things are wonderful, but none of them, even the most spiritual of the items, will ensure lasting peace.

I spent the decade of my twenties desperately seeking to control my mind. It was a valuable pursuit, but it ended in a pile of rubble. I had my first child and found myself in a mental breakdown the year that I turned 30. Thankfully, this collapse led me to a true understanding of who I am and, coincidentally, who you are, which is why I am here writing this book.

There are a lot of books on the market about mental health problems and how to "heal" them. A lot of them provide really valuable guidance. They talk about how you are not your thoughts and how your thoughts are not meaningful. While these are extremely important concepts to grasp, and I will talk about them here, they are surface details that don't reach the point of key understanding. The point of key understanding is seeing the nature of our true identity. Once we start catching glimpses of the love and intelligence that we truly are, then we can finally feel safe, perhaps for the very first time. Then the endless variety of thoughts and feelings that flow through us no longer seem important. We finally realize that they never were. Seeing who we truly are not only unravels the power of intrusive thoughts, anxiety, and depression, and any other mental illness, but it also transforms a person's understanding of themselves, everyone else, and life as a whole. In short, it changes everything.

CHAPTER 2
MY STORY

Before I tell you my story, I want to say something. You can completely skip this section if you are not interested in my story. The rest of the book stands on its own without this bit. I included my story because I wanted to give you the opportunity to see one example out of 8.2 billion of how upbringing and experiences shape mental experience. Your own experience is likely nothing like mine. However, your mental landscape and my mental landscape were both shaped by our own unique experiences. So don't read my experience and then toss the book aside because our childhoods have nothing in common. Similarities and differences between our stories are irrelevant. Let my story show you one example of the formation of a mental landscape and thought patterns. Then perhaps take some time to consider how your own story might have influenced your own landscape and patterns. And as I said before, feel free to skip it altogether.

I have been troubled by my thoughts and, coincidentally, by mental illness for as long as I can remember. I grew up in an extremely conservative religious household where well-meaning parents taught me that my thoughts were very important and that a judgmental God was always monitoring them. Coupled with this was the teaching that, along with bad thoughts, bad feelings were also unacceptable—feelings like anger, jealousy, and pride (confidence). As a result, I learned to live on edge and on guard when it came to my internal world. I repressed any feeling that was not "nice" and anxiously monitored my thought space for things that I shouldn't be thinking (based on my conservative religious upbringing). By the age of eight, I had even started having regular stomach aches, which were brought on by me thinking "bad" thoughts and then feeling extreme guilt about having them. I even developed the habit of confessing the specifics of these thoughts to my parents because that was the only thing that would relieve the stomach aches. I would pull one of my parents aside with tears streaming down my cheeks, and in a choked voice, I would blurt out the details of my offensive thoughts between sobs. My parents, usually my father, would give me a hug and tell me that God forgave me and maybe even that I really didn't have to confess everything to him. He was very caring towards me, but he wasn't able to teach me that I didn't need to be afraid of my thoughts. I think my behavior on the whole seemed like a positive thing to my parents because they were fixated on the problem of "sin" and the necessity to "try to please God." They saw this kind of behavior as me having an "oversensitive conscience," and they weren't concerned with helping me to overcome it.

Actually, the occurrence of these stomach aches and the compulsive need to confess my thoughts was the first time that I started sitting on the sidelines of life in an endeavor to monitor and gain control of my internal world. I can remember one specific time when I was in the throes of a terrible stomach ache, and I was feeling miserable and terrified because of something I had thought. My grandmother was going with her friend to a Christmas fair where all sorts of festive crafts and trinkets were being sold. That market sounded like pure magic to my eight-year-old self, but my stomach was hurting too much, and my mental world felt far too scary, and so I told my grandmother that I didn't want to go. She acted disappointed and a bit confused, but saw that there was no way of convincing me otherwise and left. I stayed home, confessed my thoughts to my mother, and remained cooped up in a room instead. There were many instances of avoiding life like this one, but that Christmas market was particularly memorable.

As I mentioned, the beliefs handed down to me as a child precipitated this behavior, but I am thankful to say that I now see that my parents had the very best intentions in everything they taught me. They were teaching me religious principles that they believed would save my soul. However, the result was a largely stressful and melancholic childhood. My once again well-meaning parents chalked that up to brain chemistry because of our family's history of mental illness. I won't go into the details of every family member, but the one who stands out the most is my late paternal grandfather, Lloyd Keen. Lloyd was diagnosed with schizophrenia not long after my father was born. He was in and out of a Shands Vista, a psychiatric hospital which is now known as UF Health Shands Psychiatric Hospital in Gainesville, Florida. Lloyd took his life by suicide when my father was about four years old.

For every "mentally ill" family member in my family line, there is a whole story behind their diagnosis. I'm sure I don't even know the half of it. However, based on what I do know, the symptoms make perfect sense—not as a genetically inherited mental disease, but as perfect outputs of the circumstances and learnings of the individuals. For now, I will focus on the story of my grandfather, because I think it's important to see how, even in the case of the diagnosis of schizophrenia, the mothership of all mental illnesses, the output is an appropriate expression of the inputs.

The story goes that Lloyd was a constant disappointment to his father, who wanted him to be entrepreneurial and to take on the family business of selling commercial grocery scales. Lloyd was an academic and loved science and wanted nothing to do with running a business. Early in his adult life, Lloyd served in the Air Force during WWII in Germany, and while he was there, he impregnated a woman. So little is known about this event. We don't know if he loved the girl or if the pregnancy was the result of a fun fling. But when he came home, his parents (my great-grandparents) were adamant that he cut ties, send the girl some money, and pretend that it never happened. That isn't what he wanted, but he complied. Shortly after, he met and married my grandmother. They had two sons, 13 months apart (my uncle and my father), and tried to do life together in Miami, Florida. My grandmother told me once that he was ridden with guilt about the girl and the child who were back in Germany. He started to struggle in life, and the story goes that his mother, Maggie, would try to take care of him by helping him convalesce. My grandmother said she (Maggie) would put him to bed, kind of like a child. Consequently, the care that he received further separated him from his daily life and family. As is natural when one starts to disconnect from real life, responsibilities, and relationships, Lloyd continued to deteriorate. He was very preoccupied with his "sins," which is also natural as someone who was raised in a conservative Baptist home where sexual abstinence was violently preached, who impregnated a woman from an enemy nation, and whose illegitimate child was left in God only knows what circumstances across the world. So yes, he was preoccupied with his sins—surprise, surprise. And he continued to deteriorate and started having what appeared to be hallucinations where my grandmother would find him standing over the stove, where he was searing the hairs off his arms, believing that they represented his sins. That was when he started going to Shands Vista to receive treatment. He would see his wife and kids intermittently, but mostly lived with his parents. It has been said that he was afraid he wasn't worthy of being a father. He shot himself and died shortly thereafter, leaving my grandmother, two sons, and broken-hearted parents behind.

This is not a book about my grandfather, and it isn't a book specifically about schizophrenia. However, the tragedy of my grandfather's story is an enormous catalyst for my work. There were a lot of very good reasons for Lloyd to start struggling at the time that he did. I believe that if he had had access to the information that I have now, his story would have gone quite differently. Instead, religion focused on sin and God's judgment and science that slapped a fatalistic diagnosis on him and attempted to help him with harsh treatments and side-effect-ridden medication, made it so that he believed that he was better off dead. If you ever hear of someone diagnosed with schizophrenia, or if you fear becoming schizophrenic, remember this little story. Mental illness isn't some sort of mysterious switch that gets flipped. There is always more to the story.

Now, back to my story. I am convinced that my own anxiety and melancholy had nothing to do with inherited brain chemistry and everything to do with the teaching and conditioning that I received. The output of intrusive thoughts, anxiety, and depression was a natural and intelligent product of the inputs. In fact, I have found that things almost always work that way. The output or result is always an intelligent product of the input. A positive example of this can be seen in the life of my husband. He is the oldest of four boys, born to a young couple in Bogotá, Colombia. He was (and still is) the apple of his parents' eyes as the ideal version of a Colombian boy—boisterous, soccer-loving, and extroverted. He received copious amounts of positive reinforcement as a child from both of his parents (who love to talk, by the way). At least, that's how he remembers it, and I believe him because that is how they still talk to him today. If you ask some of his older female family members who helped in his upbringing, they will tell you that he was a little terror. However, according to his mother, he was "muy tranquilo," or quite calm. Not surprisingly, my husband has done quite well for himself by most societal standards. He is confident, not afraid to go after what he wants, and has no doubt in his intellectual ability.

Another area of life where I've seen the output reflect the input is with health and fertility. My husband and I tried to get pregnant for over two and a half years before we conceived our first child. Prior to this struggle, I had always enjoyed a typical American diet full of plenty of inflammatory foods and somewhat lacking in complex nutrients (aka lots of bread, cheese, and sugar). After struggling for a while, both my husband and I started to clean up our diet, and even though we were planning to do IVF, we spontaneously got pregnant on a trip to London shortly after our first consultation with the fertility specialist. Of course, I know that this doesn't always happen, but it was my experience. The output was a result of the input.

So let's talk about some of my inputs during childhood. Repressive teaching, specifically about thoughts, was one contributor to my mental shit storm.

The other was an intense learned distrust in myself—my judgment, intuition, and overall ability to navigate in the world. I was always working very hard to make the "right" decision, but my parents had a lot of external standards, such as being nice and not rocking the boat, that my natural inclinations would often bump up against. I can remember once being at a new church where my father was interviewing for a job. My brother and I were in the children's class, and a bossy young girl (who would ironically be my best friend for the following ten years and the maid of honor in my wedding) was dividing everyone up into two teams, and she separated me from my brother. My brother was only six at the time, and he felt afraid, so I told the girl that she needed to put him and me on the same team. The girl refused because it wouldn't be fair. I wouldn't back down either, and there was a bit of a conflict that was reported to our parents. When I got home, I was reprimanded and forced to look up the girl's phone number in the church directory to call her and apologize for my actions. Instinctually, I had taken action to protect my vulnerable little brother in a foreign environment, and as a result, I was reprimanded and placed in a position of humiliation, forced to apologize for what I knew was the right thing to do. Naturally, this experience trained me to think A LOT before I acted and to always choose the path of no conflict, even if it went against my values. Now, I feel like it is worth saying that I am fairly certain my parents would not repeat this decision today if they were given the chance. They've made mistakes and grown just like I have. However, I record the experience here because I want you to see how mental conditions are created. They are not mysterious mutant genes. I wasn't born a passive, people-pleasing pushover. The output is a logical reflection of the inputs. You can look at my story and specifically my obsessive fixation on my thoughts from a psychological perspective and say, "Oh wow, that poor girl has a terrible case of OCD!" And you would be right (based on the definition). However, I think it is way more accurate, and powerful, and helpful to see how the learning that went into my body and mind produced a state that was sub-optimal.

My parents believed wholeheartedly in the principle of humans being born sinful, truly bad to the core. I internalized this teaching as: Humans have little to no inner goodness or wise intuition, and their only internal compass is a "conscience" that somehow comes from God with the purpose of generating guilt feelings when they are doing something "bad." Consequently, I learned that all of my natural inclinations were tainted with bad. I learned that I couldn't trust myself and that my only hope of navigating the world was through rigorous spiritual "work" like prayer and reading spiritual texts and by looking to external spiritual authorities to tell me what to do. I also learned to look to my "conscience" for day-to-day guidance. That translates into being very attuned to feelings of guilt and fear and making decisions based on those very heavy and self-focused sentiments. Even a decision as simple as choosing which leftovers from the fridge I wanted for dinner felt extremely complicated. My mind would feverishly go through the list of our family members, trying to figure out who would want what. I would feel very guilty if my choice meant that another family member didn't get what they wanted, and I would intentionally choose whatever would most likely keep that from happening. It was also impossible to enjoy simple things like board games or fun competitions at school because I was overcome with guilt if (God forbid) I was to win. I had absorbed the belief that good people always come last, and so winning seemed like it must be bad. I don't know if you've spent much time with a person whose primary compass is guilt and fear, but it makes for a glum, mundane, and selfish life masquerading under the guise of self-sacrifice and martyrdom.

Another core belief that I internalized as a child was that the world was not a safe place and that I needed to remain vigilant to stay physically safe. Unlike some of you who may be reading this book, I was not violently beaten as a child. However, my parents believed in "spanking" as a necessary part of raising a child. So even though I was a very timid and largely well-behaved child, I was spanked in a very shaming way on a regular basis for everything from getting my name written on the board at school for talking in class, to talking back to my parents, to forgetting a chore like cleaning out the bird cage. Because my primary caregivers, whom I trusted and loved, were shaming me and hitting me on a regular basis for not meeting their standards, I learned that the world was not a safe place and that I always needed to be on guard. I also learned that a big part of love and safety feels like criticism and punishment because that is how I was often treated by the people who were my primary source of love and protection. To be clear, I did receive plenty of warmth and affection as well. However, the intense concern with behavior and punishment had a formative role in my upbringing and the development of my subconscious. Because of this, I naturally gravitate to places of punishment and criticism, both mentally and in the world, because that is what I learned love and safety often feel like. My inner critic has always been a highly formidable force, and I trusted its guidance for the first few decades of my life. Also, a lot of my romantic partners have been highly critical in their worst moments.

Even the first alternative healing-focused group that I was a part of, which felt so radical and progressive at the time, had a very high focus on self-scrutiny and personal repentance. It would have felt way too foreign, otherwise!

Your upbringing and conditioning may have looked absolutely nothing like mine. You may have been raised by abusive alcoholics or happy hippies. The details are irrelevant. The reason that I am giving you this personal history is to tell you that I learned several key beliefs that contributed to a tremendous amount of confusion. Here is a short list. You might recognize some of these in your own life:

- My thoughts are extremely important and meaningful.
- Deep down, I am bad and broken.
- My natural inclinations are not good enough and need to be constantly analyzed and often repressed in order to be safe in the world.
- I am not safe in the world.
- I am doomed at worst and limited at best because of my genetics.
- Punishment and criticism are big parts of love and safety.
- God is always watching me, ready to punish me when I take a wrong step.

- I am unlucky.
- The world is a largely unhappy place.
- Suffering is the natural state of this life.

There is a good chance that along the way, you might have picked up some of these same beliefs, or other beliefs that are causing tremendous pain and discomfort in your life. I am here to show you that any belief that is causing pain and suffering is complete bullshit. I am here to change how you see yourself and how you see the world.

Viewing life through the lens of these key learnings that I just told you about (and countless others, I'm sure), I gradually formed a relationship with my mind that was dysfunctional on the best days and fully crippling when firing on all cylinders. For starters, I believed that the voice in my head was MY voice and that I was constantly being judged for any wild thing that it decided to toss out. I anxiously monitored my thoughts. If I thought something that seemed "bad," I thought about it some more and then did whatever made sense to redeem myself from it. One very consuming example of this from the early years of my marriage was related to feeling jealous and insecure around my mother-in-law. When I first met my Colombian mother-in-law, I perceived her to be literally everything that I wasn't. She seemed bold, effervescent, confident, and outspoken. She could work people and a whole room effortlessly, and she did so without reservation. But her greatest offense was that she was adored and shamelessly doted upon by my husband in a way that was very foreign to my Western American way of doing things. I was consumed with wild jealousy for this woman, and I am not exaggerating in the smallest way. But it wasn't just my feelings of jealousy that consumed my conscious experience; it was also extreme guilt and feelings of worthlessness about my feelings toward her. Being around her was horribly stressful because I would feel physically sick from all the upheaval of emotion. My poor husband had to bear the brunt of it, too, because I would regularly feel furious about how he acted toward her or about his perceived "neglect" of me, and then an hour later, I would be tearfully apologizing because I felt so badly about how I felt and acted. You see, good girls don't feel wild jealousy and resentment toward people—especially toward nice people. At least that's what I believed. I can even remember one incident on a cruise with my in-laws where I made a big scene about a family photo that I was excluded from. I got in a huge fight with my husband about it that caused us to get hardly any sleep that night and to feel completely miserable the following day. It was toward the end of the cruise, and for the duration of the vacation, I was consumed with guilt about how I acted. I literally couldn't think about anything else, no matter what we were doing or seeing. So finally, on the last day of the cruise, I offered a "Hail Mary" apology to his mother—confessing how jealous I had felt and how badly I had acted. It was yet another emotional and tearful apology to add to the books. Apologizing isn't really a thing in my in-laws' family, and I think my mother-in-law was kind of taken aback by the spectacle. Deep down, I had hoped that an apology like this would make my mother-in-law feel and express lots of love toward me, but instead (naturally) she politely received what I had to say and tried to comfort me, and then everyone went about their business. I continued with my wildly cycling thoughts and emotions that I couldn't control to save my life. It was beyond exhausting and stressful.

Ironically, while I often saw my mind as the enemy and anxiously monitored its content, I simultaneously looked to it as my primary guide and compass. I told you how I learned that my natural intuition and inclinations couldn't be trusted. In fact, they were often punished by my caregivers. One example of this was when I was punished for trying to protect my brother by making sure we were on the same team at the church event. Other experiences where I learned this involved being punished for expressing anger or disagreement toward my parents. They had learned that this kind of communication from children was "disrespectful," and so it simply wasn't tolerated. If I "talked back" to my parents, I was spanked. I learned to heavily filter what I said and what I did before letting anything out, and so the dominant voice in my head took on a puritanical, critical, worried, and moralistic tone in an attempt to protect me.

Throughout my day-to-day life, my inner voice is constantly narrating. It judges me and other people. It criticizes my actions and decisions. In every conversation, it is in the background, analyzing, mulling, ruminating—constantly plotting and planning what I should say or do next in order to be okay. One of the ways this personal narrator became a problem was apparent in my social interactions. I was in the eleventh grade. I had just transferred from a private school to the local public school with the hope of "fitting in" a little bit better socially. I had failed to make friends at my previous school. The outlook seemed promising at this new school. I had been connected to a group of girls in my grade prior to school starting because of someone my family knew through our church. This group reached out to me and invited me to go out to eat with them as a nice gesture to make me feel welcome. I can remember trying to make conversation with them and feeling completely lost and out of place. They would joke and tell stories, and I felt like I had no idea what to say. In reality, I felt so uncomfortable interacting socially in the real world. I had already transferred the majority of my attention span to my mind, which was frantically trying to read the scene and figure out what I should or shouldn't say. As a result, I just didn't say much of anything. I didn't feel confident in anything that I might say, and so it was just easier to be a wallflower. Needless to say, that group of girls stopped inviting me to hang out with them after many generous attempts.

Back to this critical and anxious voice in my mind, I came to believe that this voice in particular was mine, and that it was the key to my safety and survival. Its constant anxious ruminations and disastrous predictions seemed like truly legitimate and wise considerations to take into account. Its constant moaning about its misery and lack of self-worth seemed like a legitimate story that I had no choice but to live by. Over the years, my energy became less and less directed at concrete pursuits in real life and more and more directed toward solving the complex problems of my mood and mental state. While my peers were pouring their energy into their social lives or academic pursuits, I was trying to keep those things afloat while focusing the majority of my energy on unraveling unexplained sadness and feelings of guilt. It's so simple, really. When someone doesn't feel safe in normal, spontaneous engagement in the real world, the seemingly sane thing to do is to disengage energy and attention from reality and to redirect it to an area where you feel like you have more control. For me and many other people, the energy and attention get redirected to the internal world, particularly to the mind.

CHAPTER 3
THE BIRTH OF THE SELF-IMAGE (EGO)

The human mind has this uncanny ability to convince its listener (YOU) that it is in control and running the show. It tells this story and creates this illusion because it has been taught to believe this way. Think about it. How many times, as a child, were you told by a caregiver something like, "You should have known better! You shouldn't have done that! What were you THINKING?"

Hearing these messages over and over again tells a child that there is a part of them that knows "better" (aka that knows how to please the external authority figure) and that can make "better" decisions if he or she will only look for it. Motivated by the desire to please the caregiver (which equates to survival for a child), the child goes looking for this "self" that knows better and can make better decisions. Where do they look? Well, there is really only one place to look for a self that doesn't actually exist. They go to the imagination, also known as the mind.

Biased by this teaching that they have a "self" that knows better and can do better, the child looks to the mind in search for it. And because the imagination is infinitely creative, it creates exactly what the child is looking for. ***This is the birth of the self-image***, the personal narrating voice that mentally coaches and analyzes on a person's behalf in an effort to protect them. This personal narrating voice is literally made of the belief that it has knowledge that is superior to the person's automatic reactions in real time and that its job is to keep the person safe. It is infused with the belief that it is the one choosing and deciding all on its own. It learns that sometimes it makes good decisions and sometimes it makes bad ones. It also learns that if only it thinks enough, then it will arrive at the "right" decisions (aka the ones that other people want). We will talk more about this in future sections, but it is important to note that the belief that the mind is in control and making decisions is completely inaccurate. Not only is it inaccurate, but it is a recipe for complete misery and futility. Your mind doesn't make decisions for you any more than your goldfish does. However, unlike your goldfish, the mind becomes a frantic and insane tyrant when it is believed to be in charge and responsible for life's outcomes.

This is what happened to me and my mind. It is happening to countless people with our current mental illness epidemic. Perhaps it is built into the current framework of the life journey of being a human being. The self-image or ego is born when a person naturally encounters trauma or rejection in the world. Then the first few decades of a person's life are spent believing that they are this image that voices its thoughts and opinions in the mind and trying to protect and defend it. After all, the possession of an infinite imagination that seems to be unique to humans is no doubt a superpower, but it also comes with the potential to create deep confusion.

For those of us that are lucky, at some point this mind with its self-image begins to backfire in the form of mental illness. It starts to look like the mind is broken or sick. This was my experience, and for the longest time, it didn't occur to me to question how the same mental flow could be both my safe haven and trustworthy guide AND my greatest threat and nemesis. The same mind would simultaneously create my problems of wild, intrusive thoughts and crippling feelings of low self-worth and self-criticism. And immediately after creating this nightmare, it would go to work trying to analyze it and think up a way to be safe from it all. I wonder if you have ever noticed your mind doing something similar. If you haven't, now might be the time to start paying attention. And before you get carried away on the wave of, "Oh God, I really am crazy…" let me assure you that it is the most normal part of being human in the world. Just keep reading.

PART 2:
THE MIND – WHAT IT IS AND WHAT IT ISN'T

CHAPTER 4
YOU ARE NOT YOUR FUCKED-UP MIND

"What a liberation to realize that the 'voice in my head' is not who I am. Who am I then? The one who sees that."

- Eckhart Tolle

We hear it all the time now: "You are not your thoughts." But what does that really mean? It sounds really nice—especially if you have really shitty thoughts. For a long time after I first heard this concept, it was only something that sounded nice and provided a tiny bit of reassurance. It took me a long time to grasp the vast implications of this little pithy statement. I want to spend a little bit of time considering this popular saying because when you truly see what it is pointing to, it changes everything. What if we say it in a slightly different way? Instead of "You are not your thoughts," let's take it a step further and say, "The thoughts that you are aware of are not yours and have absolutely nothing to do with you." Can you imagine? The thoughts in your head are completely unrelated to who you are. You may, at this point, be tempted to write me off as crazy and donate this book to the nearest used book-selling establishment. "How can you say that? The thoughts that I think are in MY head. Of course they are related to me! Of course they mean something about me and my mental health." And I wouldn't blame you one bit. Our culture teaches that our thought life is highly personal and completely about us. This is not surprising because that is exactly what it looks like. It looks like I am responsible for thinking the thoughts of which I am aware, but is that actually true in a way that we can prove? The answer is not even a little bit. Let's set aside our assumptions and the stories that we've been taught for just a moment.

First, let's look at the statement, "I am the one who thinks my thoughts." Can you tell me what your next thought will be? Will you think about what you are going to eat for dinner, or something your partner said to you yesterday, or how you wish you had a partner? Will you think of a sexy movie star naked or what that really overweight guy down the street looks like naked? I can answer that question for you. No, you can't. You can't tell me what your next thought will be because you have no idea. Why do you have no idea? Because you have no control over what thoughts come into your awareness—none whatsoever. Sometimes it may seem like you are actively choosing thoughts or making thoughts go away, but that is only ever a thought-created illusion. You do not control what you think. If you could, I'm sure that you, like me, would only think thoughts that make you feel good. You might flood your awareness with thoughts of a sexy movie star or visions of yourself living the life of your dreams with the partner of your dreams. Anyone would. But you can't, because you do not control your thoughts, and you do not think your thoughts. Thoughts just float across your awareness.

So then, if thoughts do not come from you, where do they come from? They are shadows that stem from experience and learning over time. The acclaimed Russian psychologist Lev Vygotsky did extensive research on how thought develops through social interaction, particularly the exchange of words. According to Vygotsky, "Thought is not merely expressed in words; it comes into existence through them" (Vygotsky, 1962, p. 231). Thoughts are ideas, sayings, and commentaries that have been heard, learned, or experienced. Thought is a constant flow of immaterial ideas that are somehow related to things that have been learned or experienced. For example, maybe at some point when you were young, you heard an adult criticize people who are career artists. "They don't take life seriously enough! Do they really think they can play around their whole lives and get paid? They all just do drugs anyway!" So that worldview and that type of commentary were planted in your imagination. Now, maybe you think something similar when you see artists. Or maybe life has shown you a very different way of seeing career artists, but that same kind of commentary comes up when you think about another kind of career, such as a social media influencer. Maybe you even have that kind of commentary toward yourself or tons of different people and things. It really doesn't matter. My point is that thought originates from something that is heard, learned, or experienced and then mutates and takes on a life of its own. All of it is completely out of your control, and all of it means absolutely nothing about you. You did not choose what you were taught or told.

So, since you are not the one who thinks thoughts and thought material doesn't come from you, and doesn't mean anything about you, having or being aware of a thought is pretty similar to being aware of anything else you might see or feel in this life. Imagine if you were to see a random dog playing in someone's front yard, and you proudly exclaimed to your friend, "That's my dog!" Your friend would probably tilt their head and look at you with a face full of confusion and say something like,

"Umm, are you sure it's not *THEIR* dog?" That is what we do with thoughts. A thought comes up, and we immediately think, "That thought is mine! It means something about me, about my character and the outcome of my future." However, that could not be further from the truth. You are aware of the thought, just like you are aware of the dog playing in someone else's front yard. Neither are yours, and neither means anything about you. They are merely things that you notice or recognize.

CHAPTER 5
YOUR THOUGHTS ARE NOT TRUE

"Don't you see? Every thought is a lie."
- Michael Neill

We've established that we are not responsible for the thoughts that we think. Another important consideration is that thought is not true. Not a single thought can be proven to be true. I'm not only referring to the thoughts of the "weirdo" who lives down the street from you, who appears to have made very poor life choices. No, I mean that not a single thought in the Universe, including your thoughts, is true. Let me give you a quick example to show you what I mean. As someone whose current primary job is taking care of my kids, I sometimes find myself thinking, "I really should be giving my kids more of my undivided attention." This thought comes up a lot for me if I'm on my phone around my kids or if I've been away writing for most of the day, and it's usually accompanied by a heavy sinking feeling with a big dose of guilt. Now, if I shared that thought with someone who is a firm believer in never using technology around your kids, they might say, "Oh yes, that is absolutely true!" However, if I shared it with someone else who works full-time and is able to see their kids far less than I am, they might look at me as if I'm crazy, and say something like, "What are you talking about? You spend a ton of time with your kids! Don't be so ridiculous!" You see, we all live in different worlds because of what we have learned and experienced. Our thoughts often seem believable to us because they come from familiar material, but to someone else, they might seem like complete lunacy.

This can sound absolutely ridiculous and even completely untrue to most people. For most of us, the first part of our lives is spent heavily invested in what we think. When we are young, our parents explain with great conviction how the world works and what we should believe. Depending on who your caregivers were, they might have done this very eloquently with warm life lessons by the family fire, or they might have yelled at you in a drunken stupor, "Never trust an Asian, kid!"

Either way, you were being programmed, being told what to believe. Throughout our childhood, we absorb and absorb and absorb what we are taught. From these teachings and our experiences, behavioral and belief codes form deep in our core. We try to act in a specific way. We try to say certain things and not say other things. Our minds judge the world and judge us, and the rules or justifications that these actions and judgements are based on come from what we have been taught and subsequently what we believe. "People should do this. People should never do that. I should always do this. I should never do that." Fill in the blanks for yourself!

I/Other people should/shouldn't:

Be nice.

Be mean.

Be rich.

Be poor.

Win arguments.

Work hard.

Fight.

Make people feel uncomfortable.

For each of these statements, individuals may hold differing opinions on what is appropriate or inappropriate. My husband, for example, likes to say things that shock the people around him so that he can experience their reaction. For example, he loves to tell his father, who owns a school and is highly concerned about our children's education, that we don't pay that much attention to what our kids are learning because we trust that they'll be educated by "the school of life." My father-in-law, without fail, always becomes flustered and starts throwing out advice and recommendations, and my husband thinks the whole thing is hilarious. In fact, he is constantly teasing his parents about things. He has no problem making people feel uncomfortable and actually derives some enjoyment from it. I, on the other hand, have never teased my parents about anything in my entire life. I have historically believed and acted on a completely different thought commentary that says I should always make people comfortable and happy. These ways of thinking and acting couldn't be more different. Somehow, our different life experiences and learnings have generated these different beliefs or philosophies of interpersonal relating. In that sense, we live in different worlds. What's even more important and interesting for the topic of this book, however, is that any mental thought commentary related to either of these opposing belief systems is not true. Yes, that's right. Neither is true, even the "nice" one. How could they be? They are simply different ways of engaging people in the world, and both can be useful in different situations.

What I'm trying to get at here is that none of the thought commentary that comes into your awareness about yourself or the world is true. It never could be. It is simply one teeny tiny angle of looking at the world that was created from one set of learnings and experiences out of 8.2 billion. No two out of the 8.2 billion are exactly alike, and no single one could be the only truth. It simply wouldn't make sense. I love listening to Michael Neill, an internationally renowned transformative coach and bestselling author, talk about this:

While on the one hand, that might sound like a recipe for disaster, in my own experience I know that the less I care what I have on my mind, the better I seem to do and the better things seem to go. So to stop believing in my own thoughts, no matter how compelling a case they may seem to be making (often of my imminent demise or the impending loss of everything I hold dear), is a breathtakingly liberating course of action.

If every thought is a lie then I don't have to take any of my thinking seriously. Because I don't have to take it seriously, I'm free to enjoy it. But if I'm not enjoying it, I'm also free to ignore it altogether. This is not "denial"—it's the natural fruit of understanding that, in the words of the physicist David Bohm, "Thought creates our world and then says 'I didn't do it.'" (Neill, 2019)

No thought is true. Not one. Each moment is an open canvas of possibility, completely unbound by the confines of thought commentary, which tends to inhibit and restrict in the harshest of ways. Letting go of the belief in the truth of your thoughts is one of the most liberating shifts that can happen. You don't need to psyche yourself into believing it; you just need to see that your thoughts could never be the one and only truth.

CHAPTER 6
THE HUMAN SUPERPOWER

What is this mind that we possess? Where is it? How does it work? How strange is this faculty that is seemingly unique to the human species? It is a channel into a world that is not concrete, one that can deliver powerful moments of insight and one that can also be a source of torture.

While the mind could be described in so many ways, its function can be summarized as this: The purpose of the mind is to make the unreal seem real. That is it. It is an unbelievable, imaginative superpower, an individual virtual reality. Think about it. You go to the store to buy someone special (your auntie) a birthday present. You see an item that you think she might enjoy, perhaps a ceramic floral vase of some sort. You pick up the vase, and suddenly you are envisioning a series of different scenes. You picture your aunt opening the gift. You picture her lovingly filling the vase with flowers and giving it a permanent home in the center of her dining room table.

You picture her saying "thank you" to you for the gift. You might even envision her not liking the vase and judging you for choosing something cheap and tacky because you remember a time when the two of you were shopping together in Target and she mentioned hating some of the decorative items. Not only do you see these different images, but while they pass through your mind, you experience them as well. You feel the emotions of love, excitement, and pride, or shame and embarrassment. You experience the imaginary as if it were really happening. All of this is possible only because of your mind or imagination (they are one and the same, after all). It makes the unreal seem real.

What about when the mind produces images or scenes that are not so tame or mundane? What if the productions of your mind terrify you? Oddly enough, the fact that you feel frightened by terrifying mental creations is a sign of mental health. It means that your imagination is working exactly as it is supposed to. The feelings might not feel very pleasant, but the mind or imagination is once again working brilliantly. It is simulating a non-reality so that you can experience it. It is because of this ability that we humans can have the experience of being disturbed by our thoughts or even petrified of them. It is also the reason for the entire health category labeled as "mental illness."

PART 3:
THE SELF IMAGE – A CREATIVE MASTERPIECE SO GOOD IT FOOLED YOU

CHAPTER 7
THE WILD CREATION OF INTRUSIVE THOUGHTS

If you're reading this book, you are probably familiar with intrusive thoughts, but let's make sure that we're all on the same page. Even if you do not feel that you struggle with intrusive thoughts, keep reading, because I promise there is something here for you as well. According to the DSM, intrusive thoughts are "unwanted, persistent, and recurrent thoughts, images, urges, or impulses that cause distress." The stereotypical intrusive thought is usually based on some sort of disturbing content. Here is a list of some of the most common intrusive thought themes:

- Sexual thoughts
- Violent thoughts
- Self-harm thoughts
- Religious thoughts
- Negative thoughts about oneself

- Suicidal thoughts
- Thoughts about being humiliated in public
- Thoughts about the demise of loved ones
- Thoughts about sickness or poor health
- Thoughts of existential quandaries
- Thoughts of going insane

This is the short list, but as you can see, intrusive thoughts can be about anything that really bothers or disturbs someone, and they have to include all of the themes that might land someone in jail, a mental institution, or dead. For example, one of the most common intrusive thought experiences that I have heard is being plagued by thoughts of driving into oncoming traffic while operating a car. The person doesn't want to do this, but the thought is so vivid and feels so terrifying that it seems like a real threat that needs to be taken into consideration. That would be an example of a classic intrusive thought. However, it is important to note that if we zoom out a bit, it would also be true to say that any mental illness, such as depression or anxiety, is, deep down, an intrusive thought issue. The anxious person is plagued by anxious thoughts, which are accompanied by feelings of panic or anxiety in the body. The depressed person is plagued by negative and low thoughts that are coupled with feelings of worthlessness, futility, and exhaustion. The OCD person is mesmerized by thoughts of checking, doubting, optimizing, or fearing, and feels paralyzed as a result. All mental illness is based in unwanted or intrusive thoughts that are connected to unwanted physical experiences.

Aside from the content, one of the key characteristics of thoughts that are labeled "intrusive" is that they are repetitive. If someone has a one-off thought that disturbs them, but they shrug it off and forget about it, we wouldn't call that thought intrusive. No, intrusive thoughts come over and over again. They tend to be so repetitive that they become an entire issue to be dealt with in a person's life, along with other real issues, like doing laundry or going to work. The thoughts are so repetitive and feel so important that "dealing with intrusive thoughts" becomes a whole new task for everyday life.

The time in my life when I was plagued the most by intrusive thoughts was after my first daughter was born. I would have thoughts about having a heart attack and dying and not being able to take care of her. I would have thoughts about losing my mind and being institutionalized and not being able to take care of her. I would have thoughts about killing myself. I would have thoughts about killing her in a violent way. I would have thoughts about losing my mind in some sort of obscene horror film-like burst of self-mutilation in front of my daughter's Gymboree class or at a family birthday party. Really, these kinds of thoughts began as soon as we were home from the hospital, and they started to gain momentum around my daughter's first birthday. I can vividly remember a specific moment around that time when I had my first intrusive thought about harming my daughter—a theme that would haunt me for years.

I was standing in the kitchen feeling quite low. I was tired, lonely, and exhausted by my continuous anxiety and my mundane motherly duties. My daughter was playing in the living room, and I was watching her while preparing lunch. I was chopping vegetables with a large chef's knife, and the thought of killing her with the knife popped into my awareness. Immediately, my body was flooded with panic. I stood motionless in the kitchen with my knife, feeling like every muscle in my body was locked. I'm sure I started praying and grabbing my phone to look up some sort of reassuring psychological resource. But nothing—no praying, no reading, no anything else that I did over the coming years—could put out the fire of terror that was ignited in that moment.

One of the many things that I did to "overcome" this thought problem was counseling. I can remember tearfully explaining these thoughts to one counselor in particular. His immediate response was, "Well, if you're having these kinds of thoughts, you should probably get some help from a psychiatrist." When he said that, I was immediately agitated. I quickly explained to him that I knew that I wasn't going to act on them, but that I hated them, and that that was the real problem. And that summarizes another key part of the intrusive thought experience. Here is a quick description based on my experience:

I have thoughts that disturb me. I don't like them, and I'm fairly certain that I would never act on them. But the thoughts terrify me so much that it's a real problem. They freak me out so badly that the infinitesimal possibility of "But what if it DOES happen?" seems valid enough to require consideration and dread.

This last bit is extremely important to point out, and I'll tell you why. Because for the person who is experiencing intrusive thoughts, there is always a sense of, "These thoughts don't fit with who I am or my values." There is also always a sense of, "I know that these thoughts are not real and will probably never come to fruition." *HOWEVER*, there is a voice in the person's head (that they believe is *THEIR* voice), and it keeps saying, "I hate these thoughts. There is something really wrong with me. What if I don't do something about this problem, and the thoughts get out of control and take over? I'm really sick and I need help." That voice is not actually the voice of the person, but they believe that it is their voice. They identify with it, and they voice its concerns as their own. In reality, that mental voice and all of its concerns are part of the intrusive thought cycle. An intrusive thought is not an intrusive thought without that disapproving and troubled voice. It's the second half of the sequence. And understanding this at a deep level truly changes everything.

The Two Parts of An Intrusive Thought

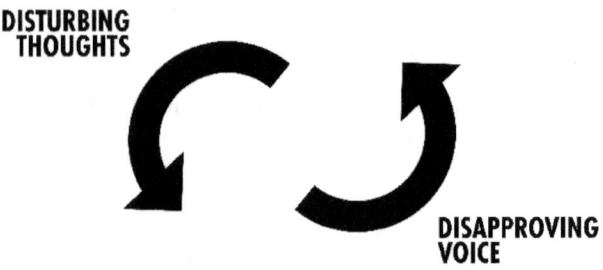

DISTURBING THOUGHTS

DISAPPROVING VOICE

This is why trying to "not care" about anxious, depressive, or intrusive thoughts never works. So often friends or therapists will advise the suffering person to just stop caring about their thoughts because they are meaningless. While it is true that the thoughts are meaningless, this guidance is often unhelpful. The problem is that when a person "tries" to follow this advice, they are often hoping that the personal narrator in their mind will finally stop saying that it cares about the thoughts. The minute the mind says, "I hate these thoughts; I can't take them anymore," the person feels like they have failed, yet again.

The truth is that when you truly realize that something isn't important, then you don't care about it anymore, regardless of what the mind says. There is no "trying" involved. It just happens. You don't need your mind to say that it doesn't care about them. Actually, you need to see that your mind saying that it hates them is just a part of the intrusive/anxious/depressed thought cycle.

To summarize, every time someone has an intrusive thought experience, the imagination presents two fabricated images. The first is the disturbing thought. The second is the "I" that sounds disturbed by the thought and feels the need to fix it. Let's turn our focus to that "I" for a bit. Believe it or not, that "I" is the real mofo. It isn't your enemy, but it's confusing as hell, and seeing it for what it is unravels the whole shitshow.

CHAPTER 8
YOU ARE NOT WHO YOU THINK YOU ARE

"You are here.
However you imagine yourself to be, you are here.
Imagine yourself as a body, you are here.
Imagine yourself as God, you are here.
Imagine yourself as worthless, superior, nothing at all, you are still here.
My suggestion is that you stop all imagining, here."

- Gangaji

I could write a whole book on the brilliance of the human mind with its power of creation and simulation. However, I am particularly concerned with a specific kind of creation of the human mind. This specific creation is universal in the human experience. It is actually the greatest work of the human mind because it is so incredibly believable, such a perfect work of creation that the mind is able to fool the real person into believing that they *ARE* this creation instead of who they really are. This is the creation of the self-image or the mental "I."

The "I" that talks in your mind is not you. Not only is it not you, but it isn't real. It is an illusion—a complete fabrication of your imagination. How could this be? If you're anything like me, you've grown up your entire life hearing that you need to learn to "find" your self, just "be" your self, and most importantly, "love" your self. While that all sounds lovely and highly productive, it is actually terrible advice. It's tasking you with the impossible—the finding and being and loving of something that doesn't exist.

At this point, something like, "What the hell? Of course I exist! What is wrong with this woman?" might be running through your mind. And you are absolutely right. Of course you exist. But all of those well-meaning teachings and pieces of advice are almost never talking about the real you. They are talking about the mental portrayal of yourself that has been pieced together over time based on what you have been told, what you have experienced, and what you have learned. They are talking about the "I" thought that blabbers on in your mind. This talking "I" is completely unrelated to who you really are and what you actually believe. More importantly, it is 100 percent a reflection of what you have been taught and what you have experienced. The "I" that speaks in your head is a tiny little symbol that represents an entire invisible cloud of information. This information consists of what people have told you about yourself, as well as assumptions that you made about yourself starting as a very young child because of things that happened to you and things that were said to you (often by very damaged people).

Let's say hypothetically that you had really mean and harsh parents. You might be relieved to finally be an adult and feel somewhat free of them. However, what you probably don't realize is that the self-image that you have or the idea of who you think you are (including your personality, habits, tendencies, etc.) is a reflection of what those parents (and lots of other sources) taught you.

Imagine a drawing of a little human figure in a thought bubble above your head. This little figure is the idea of who you think you are. If you look closer at this little "you" figure that you think of yourself as, you'll notice that every segment of the figure is made out of the written beliefs that you assimilated about yourself as a child. Some of them might be limiting but somewhat benign, like, "I am a quiet person." "I'm an introvert." "I don't like small dogs." Some of the other beliefs might be even more limiting, like "I need to keep other people happy in order to be safe" or "I need to play small because I get punished when I speak up or have strong opinions." And others might be truly crippling, like "I'm stupid," or "I always screw everything up," or "People only love me when I am sad or a victim." These are the innocent learnings of a small child. They are not true. All of these beliefs, many of which are not accessible to our conscious minds, are pieced together when we think of who we are.

The Self-Image Behind Any Thought that Starts with "I" or Ends with "Me"

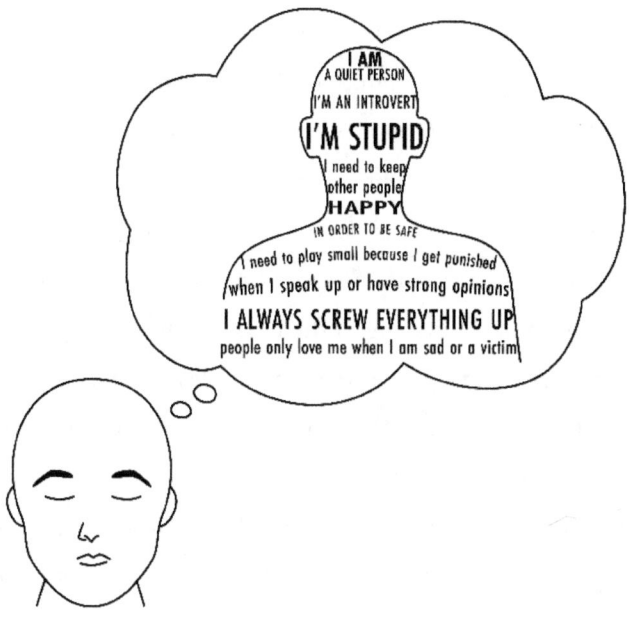

It's actually quite natural for the mind to start piecing together an image of a self even at a very early age. It's a normal and even healthy part of development. We appear to be these small, independently acting little entities. Not only that, but our little forms come with the superpower of infinite imagination. Of course, we naturally use that imagination to begin describing this seemingly independent and loner self that lives in this distinctive body. We use our amazing capability of finding patterns, conjuring up memories, and connecting dots in order to assemble a mental image of "me."

Things begin to go awry when our awareness receives external feedback indicating that we are not safe in this world, and, more importantly, that our natural instincts are not good enough. Pay close attention here, because this is very important. When that happens— when we are told directly or indirectly that we are not safe or good enough—the awareness naturally shifts <u>away from reality</u> (where we feel unsafe), from immersion in and reaction to what is happening in the moment, <u>to the mind</u> where we focus on keeping the mental idea of the "self" safe. At that point, the mind (imagination) goes to work trying to protect the image that it created. It gives advice. It identifies (creates) potential risks. It imagines potential problems and then imagines potential solutions, all to save an imagined self. It does this over and over again because, of course, there is no end to the possibilities of the imagination. Let's return for a moment to an example from my childhood that I've already mentioned. Do you remember when I stood up to the girl at the new church who was insistent that my little brother and I play on different teams, and I was punished for it after? That was a perfect example of me receiving feedback that my natural instincts and intuition weren't good enough. When I was asserting myself toward the other girl and protecting my little brother, I wasn't thinking; the actions simply flowed from my deeper intelligence. However, these kinds of natural actions were often punished in my experience (as they were that day). Therefore, I learned to stop just letting my actions flow from instinct and instead began giving my awareness to my thought world before taking action so that I could avoid punishment. Let me summarize this concept one more time, very simply, because it is so important that you see this. When we get a sense as children that we are not safe or not enough because our automatic responses are shamed or criticized by external figures or because of trauma, we naturally shift our awareness from the real world to the mind. This is why there is an enormous focus in the mental health world on mindfulness and being present. We are obsessed with this right now because many of us made that shift from being present to living in our heads.

We are now realizing that this is a problem.

Gabor Maté talks about this problem in a different but extremely compelling way in an interview that he did with *How To Academy*:

... Here's the other thing. We think that we have this one brain up here. And what's a brain? A brain interprets stimuli from the environment, processes them, and responds. That's what a brain does. So yeah, we have the cerebrum up here, but there's also— it turns out there's a brain connected to the heart. There's a nervous system that surrounds the heart which is in communication with this brain here. And of course the gut has been called the second brain; the gut has more neurochemicals than the brain does in some ways. And gut feelings are not luxuries, as we've demonstrated—they're actually a form of knowledge. So the gut is processing stimuli from the environment. When these three brains are in sync with each other, then you have true wisdom, then you have true awareness. When this one is unmoored from the other two, you can have all kinds of logic and all kinds of science and all kinds of technology, but you're not going to have wisdom. (Maté, 2022)

So many of us are living in this state. We wallow in clouds of unending logic, lost in the pondering of a desperate mind, but we are disconnected from the invaluable gut instinct because we learned long ago that it was insufficient or even dangerous because of how external authority figures reacted to our behavior as children.

But the time has come to course correct. We do not have to believe the lie that our gut instinct and consequently our automatic reactions are dangerous or deficient any longer. The only thing that is irrevocably true about yourself is that you are the force of life or intelligence fighting for its own survival in a unique form. That is how you were born, and it is the only thing that can ever be true about who you are. Yes, you might have picked up habitual behaviors in your lifelong attempt to survive. It is likely that these behaviors began precisely because of the disconnection from gut instinct and wisdom and the over-reliance on the mind with its imagined problems, judgments, and solutions. You see, that mind that most of us started giving our attention to long ago is always giving advice with the primary aim of helping us to avoid discomfort. We'll talk more about why this is the mind's goal shortly, but for now, we can acknowledge that much of the mind's guidance isn't the best because of this underlying objective. Maybe you think too much or drink too much. Maybe you struggle with rage or can't commit to save your life. Maybe you are addicted to one or multiple substances or behaviors. However, those behaviors mean absolutely nothing about who you are. Every behavior began as an innocent attempt of life to thrive. There is no exception. Recognizing this is the first step to knowing your true identity, and consequently, it is the first step to healing.

CHAPTER 9
THE MIND DOES NOT CONTROL WHAT YOU DO

Spiritual teachers often speak of oneness and wholeness and how our suffering and confusion stem from viewing ourselves as separate. While I definitely believe that seeing the oneness of all things is one of the most amazing things that a person can see, there is a kind of separation that I think can be really helpful. This separation is the differentiation between YOU (the *awareness* of thought and the *intelligence* that is moving your body) and your mind and its thoughts. Let me say it very concisely: The "I" that talks in your head has absolutely no ability to move your body in any way or to make you do anything at all. The one who moves your body is the one who is aware of that "I" voice, who also happens to be the force of life that I was talking about just a minute ago. You are aware of your mind and its thoughts, but you are not your mind or the voice that speaks in your thoughts.

It might seem a bit terrifying to hear that the "I" that talks in your mind isn't in control of anything. My God, then who is flying this aircraft of a body anyway?! What is keeping me from crashing? Well, it really isn't frightening. It's actually the most secure, most freeing thing in the world. You, the real you, are the intelligence that lives in every body that has ever breathed or moved on this planet. You are the force that animates the inert pile of materials that make up your body and that keeps the Earth spinning on its axis.

So many people have attempted to describe this force, this energetic presence that you are. Some call it love. Some call it life. Some call it intelligence. It (you) is undeniably all of these things. If I had to summarize it in one statement, I would say that it (you) is the force that is unreservedly and irrepressibly devoted to the preservation and flourishing of life in whatever form it inhabits. The infant who cries because she is hungry. The emperor penguin who endures violent blizzards with a little unhatched egg tucked between his feet. The mother who defies the laws of physics and lifts a car to save her child. This is life fighting for life. And this same life is the life that also lives in you.

PART 4:
THE ONE TRUTH – THE INTELLIGENCE AND LOVE THAT YOU ARE

CHAPTER 10
ALL THE VOICES THAT ARE NOT YOU

I want to take a minute to clarify what I mean when I say that the voice or voices in your head that speak in the first person are not truly you. Most people can relate to having a personal narrator in their head that acts as a commentator throughout daily life. It might voice opinions or preferences. It might shoot out self-criticism. It might voice goals and offer coaching on how to achieve them. It might even wallow in misery and despair about how you feel like you will never reach your goals. This commentary might always sound like the same voice (your voice) or it might even sound like different voices depending on the situation. Picture some of these scenarios:

- You go to lunch with the team from your office and your annoying coworker sits next to you and chews with his mouth open throughout the meal. The voice in your head pipes up, "Oh my gosh, he is the worst!

I can't believe he still has a job here."

- You go out with your friends on Thursday evening and have one too many (again). Then you sleep through your alarm on Friday morning and miss the morning meeting at the office (again). As you drive in a frenzy to work, the voice in your head rages, "I can't believe I did this again! I'm such an idiot. Why am I such a screw-up?"

- You walk by a person at the beach who has an amazingly toned body and who clearly dedicates time to their health and fitness. You look down at your own figure, and your narrator starts planning, "That's it—I'm going to start taking my health seriously. Starting today I'm cutting sugar, alcohol, and carbs, and I'm joining the gym when I get home."

Most of us have identified with that voice or those voices for so long that even when we begin to see that we are something more, we still get hypnotized into identifying with certain kinds of voices that say specific things. Let me explain. For some of us, it might be easy to see that we are not the voice in our head that says REALLY outrageous things. But how about the voice that chimes in AFTER the really outrageous one? Let's break this down a bit. Quite often, with any sort of thought-based "mental illness," there are several waves or phases of commentary that come together in a consecutive pattern.

- First, we become aware of the voice that says something really dark, anxious, or depressing. This might also be just an image or scenario rather than a voice.
- Second, there is often a voice of shame or condemnation: "My God, I am so sick for having thoughts like this." Or "I cannot believe that I am still thinking this way."
- Third, there is a voice that tries to dissociate from the thoughts, "I really hate this." Or "I can't take this anymore."
- Fourth, there is usually a voice of problem-solving: "I seriously need to just focus on the present moment." Or "Okay, I'm definitely going to sign up for the course on intrusive thoughts or anxiety so that I can get some help."
- Finally, there's usually a voice of self-reassurance: "I know that this is not really me. Remember you read that these thoughts are completely meaningless?" and "It's going to be fine. You really are a good person. Look at how much good you do for other people."

The Intrusive Thought Cycle

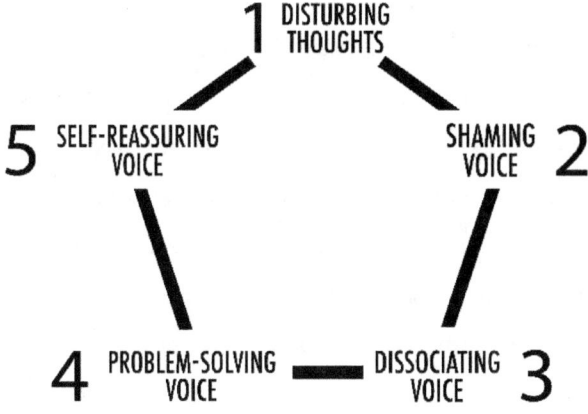

This might be a typical thought sequence for anyone who considers themself to have a mental illness such as OCD, anxiety, or depression. It might happen once a week, or it might feel like it's happening on repeat for all your waking hours (maybe even in your dreams). What is so important and so amazingly freeing is that the voice behind ALL of these comments is not you. I'm talking about the voice that says, "Oh my god, I cannot believe that I still feel this scared after I've thought that same thought a thousand times." I'm also talking about the voice that says, "Remember, none of the thoughts that you think are personal or mean anything about you." I'm also talking about the voice that says, "This whole problem isn't even real, and I just need to focus my attention back on reality."

Quite often, it's very easy to start seeing that the "terrifying" and "negative" thoughts are not you, but then, when the mind starts throwing out little gems of wisdom, we subconsciously get hypnotized by it once again. When the mind says things that we agree with, it feels so comforting and soothing to daze out and just listen to its reassuring words. It makes us feel protected because we have always felt too unsafe and exposed in day-to-day life. That is why this whole "mind problem" began in the first place. The mind runs in tail-chasing circles to distract us from reality. Because of the way we were treated by our caregivers and probably others as well, we learned that real life was perilous and that we couldn't trust our natural instincts. And to help us survive and feel safe, the mind put together a self-image that appears to have the power to make decisions, change course, and fight on our behalf. But the problem is that this self-image is made from that sense of fear, inadequacy, and unworthiness. The sense of feeling wrong and not enough was its birthplace.

Once it is born, the self-image that speaks in first-person pronouns begins to comment on everything that happens in real life. You might be having a conversation with a friend, and the voice is a constant noise in the background: "Should I bring up the fact that she didn't return my phone call? Better not—she might get mad at me. I want more coffee. Should I get up and order something, or would that be rude? I don't have much to say...I wonder if she thinks I'm boring. That laugh that she just let out—it sounded fake. I wonder if she actually likes me or just has nothing else to do on a Saturday." That is an example, but of course, the content will be different for every person.

And the mental narration doesn't only comment on the happenings of our daily life. Because the mental self-image is a reflection of our deepest fears and insecurities, it can never be at peace. It has to be constantly assessing, scheming, and planning. It is only relevant when it appears to be fighting on our behalf, so when there isn't a real problem in reality, it simply invents a problem to solve. These problems are, of course, based on the information that it has, which consists of our psychological conditioning, our deepest fears and insecurities, and the people and situations in our lives.

The misunderstanding that we began to believe long ago, the learning that we are somehow broken, wrong, or inadequate, is completely intangible and utterly unsolvable. It is a lie that casts a discolored film over everything that we perceive, creating a distorted reality where we suffer immensely. Therefore, by going to work to create problems that seem more concrete, the imagination attempts to make something elusive and unsolvable more tangible and resolvable.

The Imagination (Mind) Makes Up Problems based on Untrue Subconscious Beliefs

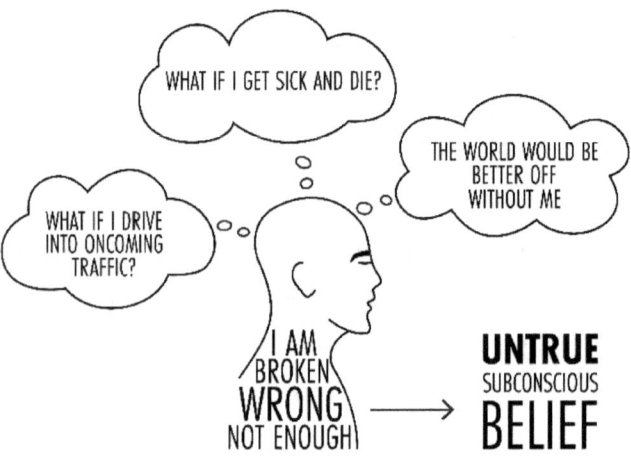

And it doesn't stop there! The imagination not only creates a palpable problem; it also creates an image of an individual person to resolve it. That is why the thoughts of people with depression, anxiety, or OCD almost always follow a similar sequence. They always begin with the problem (dark, scary thoughts) and then flow through various steps or stages of mental processing. Then they end with a wise voice (that sounds like our voice) that offers the greatest bit of wisdom that is accessible to our mind. And usually, at this point, we feel so much better. We might even feel a little bit of a high because we believe that we are finally safe again. We find temporary relief from a deep sense of being wrong. But the whole thing is made up. It is a mind-created problem.

Isn't it so breathtaking how even these "problems" are an attempt to protect our little lives? The mind, in its infinite creativity, knows that we feel unsafe and inadequate, and so it goes to work projecting images of this kind of fear and invents a "self" that we can identify with, who works feverishly to solve the problem and find a solution.

Do you know what is even crazier? For some of us, it might even be true that this mental cluster fuck actually was exactly what we needed to survive for a time. For many of us who had childhoods where we were made to feel inadequate or wrong, the distraction of mental issues AND feeling identified with a voice that works so hard to solve problems and fight on our behalf might have been exactly what we needed to keep going. Let me give you an example from my own life. When I was young, my parents believed that children needed to be highly submissive to their parents, and so any time I would challenge them or talk back to them, I was met with harsh criticism or punishment. It was much safer to not give an opinion and to stay quiet if I disagreed with something. I learned to do this in situations when I disagreed with something, but it bled over into benign situations as well. I can remember trying to do scrapbooking with my mom when I was about ten years old, and I was completely incapable of coming up with my own ideas for page designs and themes. I would just stare at my printed photographs, feeling stressed, and then repeatedly ask my mother what to do. I have a specific memory from around this time when my mother and I were attending a scrapbooking party. I was asking my mom (as usual) what I should do while she was trying to have a conversation with her friend. Her friend was getting annoyed and kind of rolled her eyes and mouthed to my mom, "I don't know how you do this with her!" It seemed like I wasn't creative when, in reality, I was terrified to make a mistake. I was paralyzed in the world of action, but my mental world was getting busier and busier. Around this same time, my mind was going full force, inventing "bad" thoughts that I would feel guilty about. I would ruminate and ruminate, and my mental narrator would try to explain why I was having the thoughts and that I wasn't really a bad person in an attempt to make me feel better. This narrator (or mental protagonist) would then come up with the best solution that it knew of to solve the problem—confess the thoughts to my parents. Doing so would make the distressing feelings go away temporarily. So while I had no solution for the suppression and paralysis that I was experiencing in the real world, my imagination was inventing smaller problems and solutions so that I could feel in control and supported. So in reality, I have always been very creative. However, all of my creative horsepower was being directed toward my mental space and the world of my self-image instead of toward real world projects. Each time I confessed my thoughts and felt better (even for a short time), it was like tying a neat little bow on my imaginary problem or like checking it off my problem checklist—giving me a false boost of confidence that I could keep going and handle things. When the external voices of other people are negative and diminishing, and when real life feels completely overwhelming and out of our control, we need an internal champion to arise. The voice that chimes in after intrusive thoughts or dark and depressing thoughts that says, "I hate this," and "I'll get through this," and that offers solutions for the problems it has invented, becomes our hero, and we become so hypnotized by it that we believe that it *IS* us.

In reality, the presence of this voice that fights for us *IS* a reflection of who we truly are, because all that we are is the essence of life in a unique form. And all that life does is fight to continue living. But the problems come when we believe that the voice *IS* us *AND* we buy into the details of what it says. Because the mind cannot only portray the force that is fighting on our behalf. Remember, the mind became such an active player in our lives to begin with because we were taught that our natural impulses and instincts were not adequate in real life. So the mind's first attempt to protect us from this inadequacy was to divert our attention from real life (where we are "inadequate") and to invent problems in the mental space that it could then work to solve.

These problems that the mind invents are always based in psychological injuries that we have held onto and that are stuck within our subconscious belief system. This is where the darkness comes in. And when we identify with what passes through our mental space, we are captivated and hypnotized by both the horror and the subsequent relief of thoughts and images created by our imaginations. To put it bluntly, we are like young naïve women with father complexes. We are madly infatuated with an older, wise-seeming professor. We blindly gaze at them, accepting everything that they say with dumb admiration and hanging onto their every word to give us advice and direction. That is the kind of toxic relationship that most of us have with the mind. But when we understand that we are the observer, part of the great intelligence that keeps our cells functioning and keeps the Earth spinning, and not the little "self" that appears in our mind and speaks in the first person, we can begin to fall out of the dysfunctional relationship. At that point, we can do two things:

1. Instead of looking to the mind to solve the dark or anxious thoughts that arise in the imagination, we can begin to see the thoughts for what they are. We will probably still feel afraid and maybe even horrified by them, but we can simultaneously feel appreciation for an imagination that is trying to be our hero by distracting us from the reality that we feel inadequate to handle. We can also start to identify some of the deep beliefs that these dark images are based upon, such as beliefs of inadequacy or being unwanted, inherently flawed, or even a victim of an angry God. This is when true magic happens because when we recognize the limiting belief that torturous thoughts are based in, and we give the whole thing gentle, loving attention, we can begin to heal the misunderstanding that formed when we were children.

2. We can appreciate the "self" voice that arises in our minds after the images of pain that appears to fight on our behalf. Moreover, we can see not only that

the voice is not us, but also that we do not need it anymore. The images of destruction are not real, literal problems to be solved. They are only creations of our imagination, an imagination that was trying to make an unsolvable misunderstanding more concrete and solvable, AND that was trying to create a hero to fight on our behalf because we believed that we were alone and broken. Moreover, when we are engaged in real life, our instincts and actions automatically happen based on all the wisdom and learning that we have believed and absorbed up to that very moment. We are not some lonely and lost pawn fighting its way in the world with only its thoughts to guide it. We are a part of the whole of the intelligence of life. And just like artificial intelligence is being programmed to do, we have been continuously learning and incorporating information into our complex webs of wisdom, knowledge, and beliefs since the first moments of conception. We are still learning and incorporating new information as we speak.

This is when true magic can take place. We stop fearing, hating, and running from our imagination's nightmares. We also stop living in a state of desperate hypnosis, waiting for the mental voice of strength and hope to chime in and solve mental problems. Instead, we realize that we ARE the essence of life, the force with infinite creativity, tireless endurance, and unending devotion to itself and its survival. And we embody that force not because we are trying to, but because that is who we are, and it is impossible to stop it. That force (which is the real you and me) has been fighting relentlessly on our behalf with the greatest love imaginable since our hearts first started to beat, and it will continue to do that until we take our final breath.

CHAPTER 11
FALL IN LOVE WITH THE LOVE STORY OF YOUR LIFE

Let me tell you something. You are so madly, truly, deeply, blindly, and hopelessly in love with yourself that you will do ANYTHING—no matter how stupid, how crazy looking, how idiotic, how mental—if it seems like it might help you make it another day. The story of the lengths that you have gone to in order to live another day makes the passion of Romeo and Juliet look boring. You adore yourself and being alive (no matter how much your mind talks about hating it). Understanding this is really important because it is one of the keys to freedom. Let me give you an example to show you what I mean. One of the categories of extremely damaging behaviors people engage in is self-harm. It's easy to look at self-harming behaviors and wonder how such actions could ever indicate anything other than self-hate. However, studies have found that even self-harm behaviors are often a misguided attempt to help the person cope. A recent study of 13 individuals who had engaged in self-harm behaviors cited many different motivations (Mughal et al. 2023). Some of the participants reported using self-harm to distract themselves from emotional suffering. Others talked about how they would utilize the physical pain of self-harm to feel grounded and connected to reality when they were feeling dissociated or disconnected. Still others talked about using self-harm because they had no other way of justifying or explaining the amount of emotional suffering that they were experiencing, and so incurring physical harm helped them to make sense of their experience or to feel as if it was more congruent. Participants also noted that self-harm behaviors helped them to feel in control when their emotions felt very out of control. One participant even mentioned that self-harm behaviors gave them an opportunity to feel cared for by themself afterward. Some participants even reported that they used self-harm behaviors as a way of dealing with suicidal thoughts and as a way of ensuring that suicidal thoughts were not acted upon. In short, the study found that self-harm was being used for the purposes of coping and self-preservation. These goals are almost always present when you really start examining destructive behavior. This particular study that I am referencing noted this motivation as concerning, but noticing this is actually a life-giving revelation when it helps a person to see that the life inside of them is always fighting on their behalf, even when the behavior appears hateful and even when their thoughts are full of self-loathing. The behavior is misguided, but the motivation is love and care.

Let's take a beat and appreciate what we just uncovered. Every single behavior you take is an attempt to care for yourself and preserve your life, even if it doesn't look like it.

It can be so incredibly difficult to see that we love ourselves when so many of our thoughts and behaviors look like they are trying to sabotage us. When we can't stop drinking, can't stop shopping, can't stop eating, and can't stop terrifying ourselves with our thinking, it really looks like we hate ourselves. But I promise you that this couldn't be further from the truth.

You see, the human system is a masterpiece of design in self-preservation. The intelligence or life that you are is always automatically reacting to reality in real time in the best way that it can, based on what it has learned over the history of your life. In other words, in addition to all the unhelpful beliefs that you might have picked up through your childhood, you also gained a lot of wisdom on how to survive. This storehouse of wisdom includes biomechanical skills such as how to walk and how to drive a car. It also includes more complex and situation-specific survival tactics, such as learning to stay small and quiet to avoid the wrath of a parent with a rage problem. The life that you are draws on this bank of wisdom in every moment that it responds to reality. This is why you can think a thought about driving into oncoming traffic while you are driving on the highway, and you still don't do it. Because your mind isn't driving the car. The life that you are is driving the car, and it acts based on all the survival wisdom that it has stored behind the scenes.

Of course, the question then arises: Why do we think or do things that harm others or ourselves over and over again? The answer is always the same. It is because we believe the content of the mind AND because we believe that it is always in our best interest to avoid discomfort (more on that in later chapters). The poor little self-image of the mind tries so hard to be our hero, but its advice and suggestions get us into so much trouble because they are based on the belief that we are wrong and inadequate. That's why the mind of an alcoholic constantly rehearses her pain and then urges her to get a drink: "Today was really hard, you deserve it." The chronic overeater wallows in a haze of self-criticism and dark thoughts of depression, and then a comforting motherly voice chimes in that says, "Just one more doughnut won't make much of a difference." The person who believes they suffer from chronic anxiety rehearses a familiar series of terrifying images until finally a gentle voice comes to the rescue with some sort of advice: "I shouldn't drive in this condition; it would be better for me to just stay home."

All that the imagined self-concept can do is walk us through its imagined problems and then offer advice for a broken and deficient person, because it is made from that belief. So yes, following the advice of the mental voice will almost never lead us to thriving or success because it is made of the belief that such things are not possible for us. The voice that speaks in first person in our mind is not us, and it is also not our true hero. It is the creative invention of the mind of a child who was told that they are not enough or that something is wrong with them. Everything that it says is made from that belief.

The intelligence that you are never stops fighting for you. However, what seems like the best choice or action can have very poor outcomes when the content of the mind is believed. Of course, when our infatuation with the mind begins to fall away and we stop looking to it for moment-to-moment guidance, the intelligence that we are becomes more and more free to act from pure wisdom and intuition. Once that starts to happen, anything is possible.

CHAPTER 12
YOUR PROBLEM DOESN'T EXIST

Let me tell you something really important. Are you paying attention? Okay, here we go:

You are not really afraid of anything. You are just afraid.

Let me say it again. You are not really afraid of anything. You are just afraid. This is important because the entire experience of mental illness is based on this misunderstanding. Let's look at a few examples so that I can show you what I mean.

First, let me tell you a story about my own experience with anxiety. I had a lot of complications shortly after the birth of my first child, and I was in a very weakened state when I got home from the hospital. As is the case for most people who are being discharged from the hospital, I was sent home with a list of things to "watch out" for, symptoms that could indicate infection or other complications. I felt extremely worried about the state of my health. I started vigilantly monitoring how I felt and anything that seemed "abnormal." I was extremely preoccupied with the fear that I might not be able to take care of my daughter, and I started to fixate specifically on my heart rate because I had heard that heart problems could arise because of the birth complications that I had experienced. Before I knew it, I was waking up with heart palpitations, buying blood pressure monitors that tracked my vital signs, and compulsively pressing my fingers to my neck to check if my pulse felt "normal." I also started avoiding leaving the house for fear that the exertion would be "too much." I even reached a point where I was afraid to shower because washing my long hair seemed like it might be too much for me to handle. And let me be clear, it wasn't that I didn't want to do these things or that I was lazy. I was literally terrified of over-exerting myself and having a heart attack. It sounds insane now, typing it out on my computer, but back then, it looked as real as my hand in front of me. However, I now know that I wasn't truly afraid of having a heart attack or of over-exerting myself in the shower. Let me explain what was really going on.

I had a cavern of fear inside of me that gathered throughout my childhood. I didn't know it at the time, but it was always present, pulsating below the surface and driving my every decision and action. This fear is the electrical or energetic charge of the faulty belief of being flawed, insufficient, and unsupported. This kind of belief has to have this "negative" feeling or resonance because it goes against the nature of life. In very simple terms, the feeling of a false belief like this has to feel bad because it is the antithesis of life, the opposite of truth. When my very controlled existence was rattled slightly by the traumatic birth, a small crack was formed, exposing the cavern. Consequently, the fear that had always been there, secretly driving me below the surface, was exposed. When that fear was exposed, my mind dutifully went to work putting words and images to what I was feeling to help me try to make sense of the feeling. But the words and images coming from my mind were not true; they were (and still are) just creations of my imagination. It's like my body and mind are on the same team and participating in a game of Pictionary. My body is the drawer and produces a drawing in the form of a feeling. My mind or imagination is the guesser and spits out words and images that seem to fit. And even though the body and mind are always trying to work together for our benefit, the efforts of the mind can be incredibly confusing if we don't know that feelings of fear or sadness or rage that are disproportionate to the current situation ALWAYS stem from a subconscious belief that originated before conscious memory even though the mind attempts to interpret them in the context of the present moment. So, back to my postpartum experience. I wasn't truly afraid of having a heart attack. I was just afraid.

The Body and Mind's Game of Pictionary

Similar to this anxiety example, when we have "intrusive thoughts," we believe that we are afraid of very specific things. First, we believe that we are afraid of the content of our thoughts. For example, if we have intrusive thoughts about hurting our children or of driving into oncoming traffic, we believe that we are truly, deeply, completely afraid of those things. Some people believe these stories to such an extent that they begin avoiding people or situations in real life related to the fears (e.g., their children or driving a car). This belief that we are afraid of these things seems completely logical because that is how it feels. Often, we might experience a thought, and immediately, our body is gripped with sensations of panic.

When we suffer from intrusive thoughts, this experience happens over and over again. The same vivid images appear at different times and in different places, and the full-on panic experience washes over our bodies with chilling fury. It is all-consuming and feels like the most important thing in the world. Immediately after, the judgment pours in. Why am I thinking this? What is wrong with me? What if this never stops? What if the thoughts get stronger and then one day I actually do what I'm so afraid of? What if I get put in an institution or charged for murder? What if I die? The nightmare scenarios are endless, and the mind, in all of its imaginative and creative power, gets center stage like a really bad actor that just can't get enough of his own voice. And when it's all over, what are we left with? Well, nothing really, except for more entrenched beliefs about how messed up we are and how truly terrified we are of whatever the intrusive thoughts portray.

The reason that I can talk about this with so much color and conviction is that I have true, firsthand experience. I've had intrusive thoughts for my entire life. In fact, you could call me the queen of intrusive thoughts. They've caused me lots and lots of grief over the years. You could even say they've been a constant experience. However, one thing has changed more than you can imagine—the content of the thoughts. The content has changed a million times based on my age and what happens to be important to me at the time of the thought.

Let's take a walk down memory lane so that I can show you what I'm talking about. When I was a little girl, being raised in a very conservative Christian home, I had intrusive thoughts about cursing at God and burning in hell forever because of it. There is a little verse in the Bible that goes like this: "And everyone who speaks a word against the Son of Man will be forgiven but the one who blasphemes against the Holy Spirit will not be forgiven." (Luke 12:10)

Of course, ideas like this are the perfect fuel for intrusive thoughts. Unforgivable sins that involve vague terms such as "blaspheme" could land you in a pit of never-ending fire for all of eternity. I mean, it doesn't get much scarier than that. So I (and apparently a lot of other Christians, according to Google and lots of random Christian websites) was terrified of accidentally committing this sin. I can remember being about 13 years old and sitting inside the church where my dad was working while I waited for him to finish teaching a class. I am fairly certain that there was an activity that I could have been doing with other kids, but I was too weighed down by my chaotic mental experience and had no energy to socialize. I had come across the verse that I just mentioned in my personal Bible study, and to my horror, my mind was frantically inventing vivid ways to curse the Holy Spirit. Of course, immediately after these thoughts, it would frantically go to work confessing my sin and asking forgiveness. It was torture. I felt lost and terrified of the eternal destruction that I might be up against. I think it's rather common knowledge that if you desperately try not to think about a certain thing, you will only be able to think of that thing. However, my young self either hadn't heard of that concept or couldn't quite grasp it.

My childhood was frequently haunted by this sort of thing. I have a memory of one of my caregivers telling me that if I thought a "bad thought" and didn't confess it to God, I could go to hell. So my young little imagination would come up with every "bad" thought that it had the subject matter for. I was haunted by thoughts of me cursing in my head, thoughts of hating my little brother and not wanting him to come home from the hospital, thoughts of being attracted to girls instead of boys. These are just some of the ones that I can remember. I would think the thoughts, feel terrified, and often confess them to my parents , who would usually try to help me feel better. Still, I usually felt miserable afterward. I can even remember a particular moment when I was between five and eight years old and my parents were watching Wheel of Fortune on television. The thought popped into my head that Vanna White (who was probably in her mid-thirties at the time) was more beautiful than my mother. I was immediately overwhelmed with guilt and ran to my mother to confess. Poor little me! I missed out on fun outings with my family and lots of get-togethers with friends. Quite frankly, starting at a very young age, I just missed out on life in general. Instead of being present with whatever was going on, I was often lost in my troubled thought world—desperately trying to make sense of it, fix it, and free myself from it.

When I got married, I would have intrusive thoughts about my husband being attracted to other women. Anyone who had qualities that I perceived to be better than mine (aka his high-performing, audacious co-worker or even his mother) was a potential threat—even if it made zero logical sense. And once again, these thoughts didn't just involve a little thought and little discomfort; they involved countless hours of miserable sensations, missing out on lots of activities and events because I just didn't want to deal with the mental turmoil, and hours and hours of judging and hating myself for having the thoughts and feelings in the first place. In addition to all of this, let's not forget the countless hours of therapy that I paid for with money and time in an attempt to fix my sorry self. The cost has been tremendous.

When I had children, the intrusive thought game of my mind reached a whole new level. Something about being responsible for keeping another little being alive put everything on hyperdrive. I started having terrifying, intrusive thoughts about losing my mind and not being able to care for my daughter almost immediately after her birth. I would imagine that I was hearing things that weren't there. I was terrified of not being able to sleep, and my poor body was so intensely stressed that I wasn't able to sleep (day or night) for over a week straight. I was constantly haunted by fears of becoming schizophrenic because of my grandfather's diagnosis.

Then these general fears became more specific. I've already told you about the day I was using a large, sharp knife, and I had a vivid thought of, "What if I cut or kill my daughter with this knife?" That experience began a fixation on intrusive thoughts about hurting my kids that lasted for years. I can still recall countless nights of being awake with one of my young infants in the wee hours of the morning and being plagued by wild imaginings of some creative and horrible way that I might kill her. Amazingly enough, I knew better somewhere deep in my being, and I kept moving and doing what I needed to do instead of running away. But the degree of panic and discomfort was almost unbearable. And these thoughts and feelings were there to greet me every morning when I opened my eyes and all through the day until I went to bed. Sometimes they would even haunt my dreams.

Although this final bout of intrusive thoughts felt as though it was going to kill me, enduring it and living with it allowed me to really start seeing through my mind's stories for the very first time. And that is a battle that I am truly proud of fighting in my lifetime, on my behalf and on behalf of my children.

As you can see, the nature of anxious worries and intrusive thoughts can include any subject matter imaginable—from taking showers to harming children. However, through all the wild stories, I find that three things always stay the same: the feeling, the underlying storyline of something being "wrong" with me, and the voice that follows the anxious ruminating or scary thoughts that sounds like it is trying to help me and defend me. The wild and incredibly detailed stories have always changed based on what is most important to me at the time. However, every story is undeniably based in my beliefs in my own inadequacy and brokenness. And—

oh my God—the feelings, the unmistakable heavy sense of dread, panic, hopelessness, and inability to breathe all rolled into a ball and stuck in the pit of my stomach or wedged inside of my throat was also a constant. Finally, let's not forget the sweet sounds of the little voice speaking in first person that appeared to be fighting on my behalf and throwing out potential solutions left and right, all the while denouncing the frightening thoughts that always preceded its appearance—the thoughts that were products of my vivid imagination just like the hero voice itself. Why have these three components always been a continuous part of my experience?

Because I am not afraid of anything. I am just afraid.

When I was a little girl, I learned in a variety of ways that there was something deeply wrong with me and that I was not safe in the world. I believe this belief resulted from religious teachings of my sin nature and innate "badness," as well as family stories and beliefs in our genetic heritage and inheritance of mental illness. There are infinite ways to learn that you are wrong or flawed, and so many of us do through unique parts of our own story. I internalized this belief profoundly, and therefore, deep in the subconscious of my psyche, there is a little burning fire of fear, of insecurity, of desperation, of not being alright. Sometimes it is a dull little flicker that lightly glimmers in the background of my experience. Other times, it is a seething, spark-spitting wildfire that fills my entire experience while reality seems to recede to a tiny speck behind it all. It has always been there, this sense of being at risk and in a very precarious situation. The feelings wax and wane, but the source is constant.

What is so amazing is that I have come to see my mind and its stories as desperately trying to explain the feelings that arise from this bottomless pit of fear. That is why the content of the story is always changing. My little mind is always drawing from whatever content appears relevant and important at the time. There is no lion to run from, no problem of starvation to solve, no enemy predator banging at my door. And yet, there is a constant burning of fear because it is a fixed part of the unconscious lens through which I see the world. My little mind and the "I" image that it created have been working tirelessly for as long as I can remember to try to solve the problem of that little burning fire of fear. But they cannot solve the fear because they are made of the same fear, the same sense of being not "okay" that they think they are trying to solve.

You are not afraid of going crazy. You are not afraid of hurting your children. You are not afraid of driving into oncoming traffic or committing suicide in some other creative way. You are not afraid of poverty or homelessness or illness or whatever story your infinite imagination has concocted. You are just afraid. You are afraid because you learned at an early age that you are not safe in the world and that you are inadequate for life's challenges. It really is that simple. Thankfully, undoing this complex web of confusion and life-sucking misery is quite simple as well. It doesn't even require complex tools or hours of work. Unraveling the web begins spontaneously when you stop watching and believing the details of what the mind is saying. We'll talk more about this in the next chapters.

CHAPTER 13
YOUR MIND WILL NEVER FIND THE ANSWER TO THE PROBLEM

So, what is one to do about this slow burn of fear that smolders deep within the unconscious? The first thing to "do" is to stop looking to your mind to solve the problem. As I said previously, the mind that talks to you all day and refers to itself in the first person ("I") is a creation of the same soup of fear that causes the thoughts and feelings that it claims to hate. They are literally one and the same, two sides of the same coin.

Anyone who has ever believed that they have any kind of mental health problem has spent a lifetime looking to their mind to find a way to feel at peace with themselves. Our minds search and search. They study spiritual doctrines, disciplines, and health protocols and different schools of psychological thought in a lifelong attempt to feel okay. As an alternative (or sometimes simultaneously), our minds suggest that we just find ways to numb the discomfort of the shitty soap opera that they have created. Then we find ourselves dependent on alcohol, television, caffeine, illegal drugs, exercising, sex, or any number of things that help to make the discomfort recede into the background for a little while. After a while, our pain and web of problems only expand, and our precious time and money are lost in a strenuous and painful world that revolves around imaginary problems.

But the same mind, the same "I" that tirelessly searches for answers to fix the problem or substances to soothe it, is simultaneously ALWAYS doing something else. It is ALWAYS coming up with new problems! It is an endless source of new things to worry about, new potential nightmare scenarios, new dire explanations for low moods and panicky feelings. It predicts destruction and mayhem, and then goes to work trying to "fix" itself for thinking those things. It is complete madness! That is because the mind, and the "I" that it portrays (as you), is a creation of the fear that bubbles deep in your subconscious. So the "I" that talks in your mind will never solve the problem of your fear because it is made of your fear! It is part of the whole program. It pretends to be something different—some sort of independent and logical voice that really will one day finally save the day. But it really and truly can't. The "I" that talks in your mind is simply an image that was created when you, as a child, first started to believe that there was something wrong with you and that you were not safe in the world. You felt lost and inadequate, and your beautiful imagination went to work creating an image of the independent "you" fighting to live another day, along with problems for this pretend "you" to "solve."

Really focus with me for a minute because this can sound a little abstract, but understanding it can be the first step in solving your mental health problems. Children do not enter the world thinking about what they should do next. For them, it is the exact opposite. They live in real time. Their bodies automatically respond with action or words based on whatever makes sense to them. This is why they are so authentic. Nothing is filtering their automatic responses.

However, once a person really absorbs the message that their automatic responses are not good enough and that the way that they do things is wrong, then they are no longer free to be fully present in the moment. They learn that their responses need to be filtered and that they will be safer in the world (safer from their caregivers or peers) if they think before they speak or act. Once they internalize that teaching, THEN AND ONLY THEN, the idea of the "I" arises. The first-person voice in our heads that judges and premeditates and tries to do or say just the right thing, depending on our personal values, wasn't there from the beginning. It was born when we learned that our natural way of being in the world was wrong or not enough. For example, I was often reprimanded and spanked as a child for "throwing a tantrum" and then later for speaking to my parents in any way that seemed "disrespectful." The problem is that these behaviors are natural for any child. So I quickly learned that my natural emotional responses and ways of expressing myself were not safe and would result in emotional and physical pain. And because I was and still am an intelligent and adaptable creature, I learned to consult my mind before acting in real time. I would filter my thoughts and feelings in the mental space first (whenever I was able), listening to the little "I" in my mind talk about what it could do or say and still be safe. Then (and only then) I would shift attention back to reality and take action.

The minute that you started to believe that your automatic emotional and behavioral reactions were not acceptable or safe because of something that someone else said or did to you, your mind came up with the idea of an independent "I" who never stopped working from that moment, trying to achieve a sense of equilibrium. It is your deepest fear and insecurity crystallized into a mental image that looks and talks like you. It cannot find peace and wholeness because it was created from a belief of being insufficient and wrong.

This is why our minds appear to be so crazy. Because our caregivers were so caught up in their own fears and discomforts and insecurities (and also simply because they were human with limited patience and understanding), they taught us that the way we did things was bad or not enough. This internalized belief then directed our attention away from reality and into our thought world, and specifically to the imagined personal voice in our minds that purports to keep us safe. The problem is that that voice is only an imagined creation of a little person who fears for their safety. When a child is constantly hearing "You shouldn't have done this!" or "You should have known better!" then it only makes sense that they start turning toward the world of thought in search of this "you" that supposedly can do better and knows how to keep them safe.

The more hostile the concrete world is for a child, the more they will go in search of a protector in their imagination, and the louder the "I" voice in their head will become. Children who are verbally and/or physically assaulted for their behavior are only being trained to run from the physical world and REALITY to find safety in an imaginary world of better outcomes. And yes, I am 100 percent including any neat, clean, and "Christian" spanking practices under that umbrella of physical assault. When you cause physical pain to a child, you are indeed assaulting their person. I don't care what whitewashed intention you sugarcoat it with. It is truly mind-blowing to me that we have come so far in society to see that domestic violence between romantic partners is not acceptable, and yet when a grown man or woman hits a small child in the name of "discipline," many people nod their heads in approval. We're not supposed to hit our friends, our neighbors, or our equally adult partners when we are upset, but we are absolutely free to hit our small, helpless children whenever we feel inclined to do so. This is completely incoherent and illogical.

My hope is that if you were also the victim of physical assault as a child, maybe you can connect with my rage and feel it on your own behalf. So many of us were abused under the guise of "love and discipline" to the extent that we cannot even feel the natural anger that is healthy for someone to feel when they have been abused. Your caregivers might have truly believed that they had the best intentions in the world in their abusive discipline tactics. But it doesn't change the fact that their behavior was abusive and that you were a helpless victim. Please get angry about that. And by getting angry, I'm not suggesting that you blame your caregivers or hate them. It's very possible that they were just ignorant. But connect with the rage on behalf of the small child who had to suffer at the hands of ignorant people in an ignorant culture. The rage will give you a catalyst to break free from the mental insanity that developed while you intelligently tried to save yourself.

Whether the rejection of your emotions and behavior came in the form of physical assault, criticism, yelling, or even silence and the experience of being ignored by authority figures in your childhood, the rejection or condemnation of your natural responses pushed you toward the thinking mind in an attempt to be safe. The irony of this is that the little thinking mind controls absolutely nothing. It has no determining power. It cannot tell the limbs of your body to move or stay still. It can scream as loud as it wants, and yet the body will still do what makes sense based on what is known and believed deep within. That is because the person in the mind truly does not exist. It is the creation of the imagination of a person who does not feel safe and sufficient in the world. The power of the beautiful imagination is hijacked, and instead of being used to create new things and solve real problems in the world, it is used to create an image of the person's "self" that can ponder its own safety and survival in a desperate attempt to feel more secure and in control.

Interestingly enough, it seems that some sense of insecurity and the creation of the idea of an independent "self" is just part of the human experience. We all feel some degree of insecurity, and we create that internal concept or illusion of independent control. However, just like everything else, there is a spectrum. The more deeply we internalize or believe a sense of being flawed and unsafe, the more intensely we become immersed in our mental world, and especially in our idea of ourselves. Ultimately, what has happened is that we have believed something that goes against the intelligence of reality (e.g., "I am flawed or not good enough"). That false belief creates a little fire of fear that burns deep within us. As a result, our mental space becomes detached from reality (where we feel incompetent or unsafe) and turns into a theatrical stage where the imagined "I" churns in a desperate attempt to explain our intense feelings of fear and unrest and to solve them or make them go away.

So we think, and think, and think. We try to think ourselves to safety. And ironically, the very thinking that we are looking to for safety only draws more and more pictures of danger, because the thinking is a projection of our learned insecurity and insufficiency. This is how mental health issues such as anxiety or OCD grow to exponential proportions, to the point that people cannot leave their homes or do basic tasks out of fear. They have thought themselves into a form of oblivion. They have followed thought train after thought train after thought train until they are viewing reality through a screen of problems invented by their own imagination, and at the center of the screen is the fragile self image with all of its needs, grievances, and vulnerabilities. And because they believe that the content of the thoughts is real and true, that screen looks just as real as any other part of the outside world.

The Screen of the Self-Image and its Problems

Distorting Reality

The good news is that once we begin to pull at the threads of this tapestry of imaginary problems, the stories rapidly begin to unravel, and once you see that the fragile self-image at the center of it all is an imagined creation just like all the other stories, the whole thing falls apart—leaving the only real and true thing that has always been—intelligence living in this present moment.

PART 5:
THE ONE UNIVERSAL ADDICTION

CHAPTER 14
A CRITICAL MISSING LINK

We have talked about several foundational components of mental health struggles at this point. We are painting a picture of how life starts to appear very precarious and unsafe, and how we begin to believe that our natural inclinations and responses are not enough to navigate the world safely. We are also beginning to see how and why we start to turn our attention away from reality and toward a mental projection of "I" or "me" that promises safety and better outcomes in the world of thought.

Actually, we're about to dive into exactly how our mental webs of thought that began with the very best intentions actually become prisons from which we cannot seem to escape. However, before we go there, there is an important link that we need to talk about that ties everything together. This link is the ability or inability of a person to endure discomfort. It's actually a concept that seems to be gaining traction in our cultural consciousness right now. You hear a lot of thought leaders talking about concepts such as "grit" and "embracing pain to get stronger." This concept is a foundational building block in the ability to have a growth mindset, or the perspective that you can develop skills and intelligence through training and hard work whenever opposition or obstacles come your way. Specifically, the word "grit" refers to having a degree of courage and perseverance in the face of life's challenges. We are becoming more aware that we need to be able to do this in life, AND that a lot of us are not very good at it. You know what's really odd, though? We ALL start this little journey of life with amazing endurance and incredible grit.

How do I know this? All you need to do to know and believe this is watch small children in a healthy and supportive environment. Actually, doing so will always tell you the truth about our true nature. As a specific example, let's talk about my current toddler, who is not yet two years old. Infants and toddlers have truly astounding grit and endurance. My 22-month-old has endured countless very painful falls and bumps in her daily endeavors to get stronger and more proficient at life skills. She has fallen numerous times while learning to ride her balance bike. When she was learning to walk, she fell and had to get up over and over again, as her little leg muscles grew strong enough to support the weight of her top half. When she was around seven or eight months old, she pushed up over and over again onto her hands and knees and shakily extended her arms until she grew strong enough to crawl.

Can you imagine how hard that must be for a tiny little person? They have to work day after day after day doing these exercises where these frail and unused little muscles grow strong enough to carry all of their body weight, all the while enduring falls and bumps and bruises, and they never ever give up! They get up and try again until they master the skill. They can't help it because their drive to develop and thrive is incredibly strong.

So we all begin life as these incredibly gritty bodybuilders, but then something happens. The people who are there to keep us safe and teach us skills start to feel threatened by some of our natural responses and inclinations for countless different reasons. Maybe our innocent, unfiltered honesty embarrasses them in front of their friends. Maybe our vibrant and unending energy frustrates our teachers who are trying to enforce quiet and "order" in the classroom. Maybe our caregivers who are drowning in their own personal insecurity or other life stressors (relationship problems, money struggles, or health issues) don't know how to process their emotions and therefore have zero tolerance for the expression of ours. Any of these circumstances (and countless others) create scenarios where our caregivers meet our natural inclinations and expressions with hostility and abusive behavior.

We already talked about how this kind of response to our natural intelligence encourages us to turn to our thought world in an attempt to find safety. However, it does something else as well. When the people who are supposed to keep us safe begin to cause us pain and suffering (which, for a child, appears as a literal threat to survival), we also begin to associate discomfort with danger. Before that, we accepted discomfort and pain as parts of our learning and development process. However, when caregivers start to turn on us and respond to our natural responses with hostility and verbal or physical abuse, we are introduced to a new kind of discomfort where our survival feels at stake.

Think about it—for a child, their caregiver turning against them is literally a threat to their survival in the world and therefore something that must be avoided at all costs. So the child begins to turn to their thought world and the imaginary "I" controller, not only trying to get better, safer outcomes, but also to escape feelings of pain and discomfort, which have taken on a new connotation of a threat to survival. And this, my friends, is the birthplace of every addictive behavior that has been or ever will be experienced by a human being.

Why is this relevant for you and me? Because mental illness is nothing more than an addiction to the mind's stories and explanations in an effort to escape the trigger of discomfort. We learn to run from uncomfortable feelings by diverting our attention away from the discomfort to the "I" in our imaginations, which always has a story ready about what our "real" problem is and how we can save ourselves from it. And all of this makes perfect sense, because we are trained as children that our natural inclinations and responses are not good enough and that there is some other force inside our heads that should know better and do better. This is how we simultaneously learn to run from the discomforts of our feelings and real-life scenarios, AND hand over authority to our mind or imagination, which talks and postulates as if it were us. And all of a sudden, life starts to get very complicated because we no longer trust the only thing that is real (natural impulses in real time powered by deep wisdom and the will to survive) and instead trust a limitless imagination that has been fed and programmed by very confused people and culture. That is the birthplace of the monster of mental illness.

CHAPTER 15
THE ORIGINAL ADDICTION

We are a generation of addicts. We're addicted to our phones. We're addicted to drugs (legal or illegal). We're addicted to shopping. We're addicted to caffeine. We're addicted to sugar. We're addicted to porn. We're addicted to sex. Anyone and everyone is addicted to something. It's a widely understood and accepted aspect of being alive today.

But with all this talk of addiction, somehow, we have overlooked the original addiction, the addiction that I believe is universal to every human being that has ever lived. The original addiction is the addiction to the mind and specifically to the idea of the independently deciding self.

What is an addiction anyway? Every single addiction, from bubble gum to blow jobs, can be boiled down to one thing. That one thing is an attempt to calm or escape uncomfortable feelings. We turn to something (a substance or experience) because we feel some sort of discomfort (boredom, anger, shame, inadequacy, sadness, etc.), and that something temporarily makes us feel better. After some time, we start craving the feeling that is achieved through that something, and that craving becomes the ever-present discomfort that we need to escape (along with all the other normal, uncomfortable feelings that day-to-day life brings up). Addiction is the continuous seeking of relief from discomfort. It is the intelligence in a human form that believes the best way to survive is to make uncomfortable feelings go away.

So let's get back to the original addiction by rewinding in time to one of your earliest memories. Try to remember one of the first times that you felt ashamed or bad or afraid. I can remember being about four years old. My little brother had been having some health problems and was in and out of the hospital. I confided in my mom that I didn't want my brother to come home from the hospital. Of course, I was tired of so much of my parents' attention going to him. My poor, exhausted mother responded by shaming me for my feelings. "That's a terrible thing to say! Why would you say something like that?" I was trying to process my natural feelings, and my mother didn't know how to help me do that and shamed me instead. So where does a child go when this happens? The answer is they go to the imagination. A young child might pretend to comfort their sad stuffy. A slightly older child will use their imagination to conceptualize their self. "I didn't mean to say something bad. I'm just so tired of Mommy and Daddy being at the hospital. I'm tired of my baby brother taking up all their time. It's so unfair that he takes all their love and attention, and there's nothing left for me." This is how the idea of the self begins to provide relief from uncomfortable feelings. It's a little retreat when real life feels too stressful or difficult—a place where we feel vindicated when we've encountered judgment and shame from the world outside.

Do you know the feeling that I'm talking about? It's that sensation of feeling incredibly stressed, lost, and inadequate, and then the voice in your head comes up with a really great self-protecting and self-preserving explanation. "I know she's mad at me about that, but I really did mean well," or "I know I shouldn't have missed that deadline, but life is really too much right now. There's nothing I can do about it." The variations are endless:

"I really am right. She doesn't know what she's talking about."

"He just doesn't understand me."

"It was the best I could have done."

"If only other people knew all the shit that I have to deal with, then they would understand."

When the mind lands on just the right one of these

assurances while the body is burning with stress, shame, or fear, it feels like total bliss. The burning cools. The racing thoughts slow down. The freezing pins and needles are replaced by gentle warmth. The body goes to cool, calm, comfort. It's a high. A blissing out. Misery escaped. It's like a warm embrace from a gentle mother inside our minds. All the pain and fear dissipate, and love is found once again.

The imagination can be so good at explaining our pain away. And when we've been feeling completely engulfed and overwhelmed by our discomfort, nothing feels better. So we quickly learn to run to the internal voice whenever life feels like too much. And then, like any addiction, we turn to the internal voice more and more because we just crave that good feeling that it can give us. Before we know it, we are spending more and more time "in our heads" rather than living and responding in real life. And the more time that we spend mesmerized by the voice and waiting for it to comfort us, the more the voice crystallizes into a personal identity that seems very concrete. The problem is that this crystallized identity isn't real at all. It isn't constantly learning, growing, adapting, and evolving like the true life and intelligence that we are. It is an idea that is formed from a powerless child trying to find safety in a world that feels unsafe.

So the mental monologue is crystallized as "our"

voice as we try to fix our problems and feel safe in an unsafe world. And it just grows in complexity from there. Our imaginations add on all sorts of qualities and characteristics that we learn about our "selves" from life experience. But stripped down to its true essence, this voice of "self" in our heads is the voice of a child trying to solve an untrue belief in being inadequate or not good enough. And what does this voice, therefore, always need? It needs a problem to solve. So it creates problems and then comes up with explanations or ideas to feel better over and over again. Often, the problems have a small connection to real life, but they are embellished and expanded in gigantic proportions. You see, for someone whose natural impulses and reactions were undisturbed as a child, any problem is typically met with a natural reaction in real time. The imagination can occasionally be useful if there are multiple options to choose from, but otherwise, action unfolds in a fluid way. However, when we learn that our natural impulses are wrong or inadequate, any challenge or problem is first turned over to the imagination for planning and consideration. In the imagination, the problems are infused with the added complexity of our fears and insecurities. The imagined "I" walks around and around these imaginary problems, going through all the details and postulating a response where it will be safe, secure, and protected. The flow of reality is paused, and an imaginary Alice in Wonderland vortex based on fear and insecurity is entered temporarily. We believe that filtering real life through this vortex will help us to avoid missteps and punishment. Unfortunately, in this misguided attempt to feel safe, we end up creating countless imaginary monsters, and those creations of our imagination cost us dearly.

CHAPTER 16
THE REAL MONSTER

As many of you have suspected for some time, we do live with an insatiable monster. However, we've been mistaken about the monster's identity. We wrongly believed that the monster is our mind, or more specifically, the intrusive, anxious, or depressed thoughts that our minds produce. No—not at all. The real monster is actually an addictive process that the mind learned to facilitate long ago. This is the process of looking to our mind to find comfort and feel secure. I'm talking about the feeling that we get when we feel like we are safe, and even better, when we feel like we are in control. Because we received feedback as children that we were not good enough and that our natural responses were not to be trusted, we began to look to the mind to make it all better. And the mind, with its infinite creative potential, has been working in overdrive ever since to try to do just that. It creates problems and then attempts to solve them over and over again. The problems that it invents and the solutions that it provides are a combination of details from real life and projections of the fearful beliefs and insecurities that reside within our subconscious mind. Because the problems are created by the imagination and based in the untrue beliefs that we absorbed as children, they are literally unsolvable. Let me say that one more time because I want to make sure that you catch it. The problems that our mind creates are not real, and therefore, they have no solution. This is why you probably handle crises in the concrete world rather well, and then hopelessly flounder in your mind's stories related to your anxiety. I can remember getting completely lost for hours (even days) in a mental discourse about whether or not it was possible that I might one day unintentionally act on an intrusive thought related to harming one of my children. In contrast, I can remember a time when one of my daughters was playing in a splash pad and stepped on some sort of unidentified insect that stung her horribly. She was shrieking uncontrollably, and her foot was turning purple. I was alone at the park with my four children, but I systematically tried to comfort her while carrying my infant and slowly moving everyone toward our minivan. I gratefully accepted a little help from a stranger who offered to carry my infant to the car. I looked up the nearest emergency room on my phone. I drove to the

ER, unloaded the children, talked to the doctor, agreed to a dose of Motrin, and then drove everyone home. It was straightforward—a series of logical, automatic responses that made sense to my inner wisdom at the time. Mental stories and drama cannot be handled well because they are literal vortexes of fear, unending iterations of the belief of "I am broken and unsupported." This is why you can spin in mental circles for hours and finally come out feeling as if you are going to be sick. Whenever you ruminate in that space, you are wallowing in a dark, murky swamp of beliefs that go against your true nature (intelligence, wisdom, love, hope, etc.), and that is precisely why it feels so bad. It is also worth saying here that while it is often said that feelings are not always trustworthy guides, I find that they are extremely trustworthy guides when it comes to discerning the nature of thought. If a thought feels good in a clear, light, life-giving way, then it is resonating with your true nature of love, wisdom, intelligence, and life. On the other hand, if the thought feels bad, that means it is agitating or even repulsing your true nature and isn't worth your time.

So once again, the problems invented by your mind are unsolvable vortexes of untrue beliefs. Therefore, when the mind cannot solve the problems, it tells us how we can temporarily escape from the discomfort that we feel. These "comfort fixes" that it suggests are almost always detrimental to overall well-being and functioning because they cater to a self-image of someone who is broken and at risk (aka overeating, overdrinking, reassurance seeking, checking, avoiding, hiding, using drugs, etc.). This function that the mind learns to perform spawns addiction and creates the perfect environment for mental illness to proliferate. Oddly enough, understanding what is going on in our minds is, in fact, the very doorway to deep and profound healing. We will explore this phenomenon more in the next chapters.

CHAPTER 17
EXCHANGING MAGIC FOR MYTH

When a small human learns to believe that the world is dangerous and that they are inadequate, they instinctively search for two things:
1. A sense that they are in control.
2. Good feelings to escape the discomfort.

The imagination can be brilliantly used to achieve both of these things. Remember the monologues that the mind tends to recite whenever we feel frightened or ashamed? Maybe you have a fight with your partner and finally storm off to another room to be alone. Immediately, the silence is filled with the narrating mind. "I can't believe he did that! I can't believe he talked to me that way! He is such a narcissist! I deserve so much better than this. I am so done with him. I'm going to ignore him all day tomorrow, so he sees how hurt I am." If we take a close look at a monologue like this, we can see how the mind is creatively working to help us feel better and feel in control. We feel better when we villainize the other person and vindicate our own position and motives. These things feel great for a bruised ego. Moreover, thoughts like these give our mental self-image a sense of control by imagining an independent choosing self that makes a plan to assert and protect itself. It seems extremely relevant to the real-life situation of the fight that we just had. However, it is completely detached from reality. There is no real-time response involved. There is only our idea of our hurt self and an imagination working to come up with ideas of how that self can feel better and stay safe. None of it is real.

For the person who has learned that life is dangerous and that they are inadequate, this kind of looking to the mind's narratives and explanations becomes extremely frequent and habitual. Life feels uncomfortable and out of control, and so the attention drifts again and again to the marvelous imagination that is so good at creating a believable story of peace and control.

And that is the start of a very big problem. Because we do start to believe it. We believe ALL of it. Our mind seems so smart and so clever at finding ways to make life manageable, and that "I" voice in our head does such a good job of voicing exactly how we seem to be feeling in the moment. We forget that the mind was and always is simply a creative tool. We believe that the mind speaking on our behalf with the pronoun "I" is actually our voice.

We identify with the mind, and we believe that it chooses and controls our behavior. In doing so, we align all our energy with the never-ending process of propping up and protecting a fragile imagined self, and we completely lose sight of the marvelous intelligence that is breathing and living us in every moment. We unknowingly trade in the true identity of universal intelligence for a fabricated self that achieves temporary good feelings from solving its made-up problems. We exchange brilliant, inexplicable magic for a mentally fabricated puppet. However, the magic doesn't leave us, and it also never stops working to protect us. It cannot leave us, because it is who we truly are. So it keeps living us and moving us, silently waiting for our minds to notice it and realize the illusion that we've fallen for. It's truly never too late.

PART 6:
A MISUSED MIND – HOW IT KEEPS YOU SMALL

CHAPTER 18
A WASTED SUPERPOWER

The confusion that I've referenced throughout this book is probably one of the greatest tragedies of the human race: The erroneous belief that the voice that speaks in my mind is MY voice and that it controls my behavior. Initially, it seems so innocent. It even seems to make sense, this identification with the talking mind. However, when the mind has been fed confusion and lies from an early age, the results can be catastrophic. For example, horrific historical events such as the Holocaust only occur because teaching and circumstances plant an idea in someone's mind (Adolph Hitler's in this case) that their pain or discomfort is the result of the presence of people of a different race. A belief like this in the imagination can expand and build upon itself, and when it is believed, it can lead to unspeakable catastrophe and suffering.

On a smaller scale, we can also look at the number of people in our culture who are genuinely afraid of their minds with their wild, anxious, or depressed thoughts. According to the National Institute of Mental Health, it is estimated that one in five adults in the United States lives with some sort of mental illness. They believe that their minds are extremely powerful, and so they hate and fear the voice when it says anything that threatens the quality of life that they want to have. Eventually, this fear and hatred of the mind can become such a prominent part of a person's life that the person begins to assume the position of the mind's victim. They feel like a powerless insect caught in the complex web of the mind's depression, anxiety, and intrusive thoughts. And it is the saddest thing in the world, not only because of the poor quality of their lives, but even more significantly because they are afraid of the single greatest superpower that they have. The very thing that makes the human species so unique is our access to the portal of the mind or imagination, where we can walk through and, to some degree, experience any idea or scenario. We have access to literally limitless creativity. This ability, in addition to the power to communicate an idea with spoken language and the opposable thumbs to put thought into action, has allowed us to create and construct in unimaginable ways. So, fearing the mind is exactly like Queen Elsa of Arendelle in Disney's Frozen, hiding away in her room and losing out in every aspect of life because she is afraid of her magical powers. Instead of using the incredible machine of the mind with all its creative potential, we live in fear of our greatest tool, believing that it can independently take away everything that we love and treasure. It is an atrocious waste.

CHAPTER 19
THE TAIL CHASE OF FUTILITY

When any sort of mental illness is present, the person often fears and hates the mind. Not only that, but that same person is usually still completely mesmerized and spellbound by the mind's voice because they believe it is their own. Remember, our imagination created the "I" voice because it was trying to save us from pain and trauma that we experienced as young children. Even though we begin to hate the voice, deep down we believe that it is our voice and that it has the power to save us. So we give it our endless attention, and in return, it gives us endless content.

Recall that this whole situation began because we realized that when figures in the outside world cause us to feel uncomfortable feelings like shame or inadequacy, the voice in our internal world has the power to bring us back to peace and happiness with a nice thought. The mind, in all of its brilliance, notices this pattern, and instead of waiting for the external world to make us feel bad, it (the mind) expedites things by taking charge of the whole process. It weaves a problem-like story that is rooted in our deepest fears and insecurities with situations and characters loosely related to real-life happenings, and then takes us on a wild goose chase of misery until it arrives at a solution-like thought. I can remember repeatedly going through the cycle of having disturbing, intrusive thoughts (and panic attacks) regarding the fear of losing control and harming my daughter. The thought would appear, along with the feelings of sickness, terror, and sheer panic. I would then mentally spin for a time, listening to the voice in my head that was shaming me for having the thoughts and then for still caring about the thoughts, and then trying to convince my mental self-image that the thoughts didn't matter. Sometimes this last segment would be enough to make me feel better temporarily. If not, the voice would throw out another solution of talking to my husband about the thoughts so that he could give me reassurance that I wasn't crazy and would never do such a thing. The release that I would get either from the mental reassurance that followed the thoughts or from my husband was a spectacular reprieve from my discomfort.

The invention of problems and subsequent solutions in the mind or imagination gives us two things. First, we are distracted from real life, where we feel broken and inadequate. Second, we get a hit, a temporary high from a peaceful feeling of safety and security—even if it only lasts for a moment. It is the age-old story of addiction. We endure the incredible suffering and misery caused by our addiction for the brief high that it gives us. And in this case, the high that we experience is the feeling of the single truth of existence that has been true of every living organism since the beginning of time. This truth is that we are whole and instinctively equipped with the greatest wisdom imaginable for navigating life. The mind takes us through the darkest of imaginary nightmares so that it has a problem to solve and can arrive back at a thought that has some resonance (even if it is ever so slight) with this truth. The thought might even be as simple as, "Maybe I'll find a cure for this mental illness tomorrow (aka hope)." If we can't find a thought that gives us that feeling, we might turn to some sort of action in the outside world to serve this purpose instead. Just like my example of going to my husband for reassurance, you might seek a good feeling in the outside world through any sort of addictive behavior or even through behaviors like listening to a motivational speaker or exercising. A single cycle of an ongoing addiction completes when we experience something, either in our thoughts or actions, that resonates with the love and intelligence that we are. We are so desperate for this feeling, because we have forgotten (through the teaching of others) that we *ARE* this love and intelligence. When you know your true identity, any feeling is fine because you know feelings are meaningless. However, when you are confused about your true identity, the quest for a good feeling is frantic and ongoing.

One of the most impactful examples of the mind taking us on this roller coaster ride is unrelated to mental health. Rather, it is in the world of goals and habits. Have you ever been caught in the cycle of having a goal set in your mind, continuously falling short, and then mentally shaming yourself for your failure? Perhaps you are dissatisfied with your job or the salary it provides, and you have thought for a long time about using some time in the evenings to apply for a new opportunity, only to find yourself binge-watching Netflix every night instead. This is an amazing example of our confusion and the mind's impotence when it is being inappropriately used. As humans, we often come up with something that we would like to change or do to live a better life. A classic example of this is being healthier. Countless people have an ongoing mental goal of something like: I want to eat better. So, they think of this goal, and the mind says, "Yes! I want to do this. I NEED to do this!" And then what happens? We don't do it. We drive by the doughnut shop on the way home from work like we always do, or we indulge in way too many margaritas at happy hour AGAIN. Then the mind storms in with a vengeance, "OH my god, I did it again. I'm such a fat ass. I can't believe that I am such a loser. What is wrong with me?"

But it doesn't stop there. Often, the mind then comes up with an excuse and then a plan. So first the excuse comes in, "It's just that I was feeling so stressed. My boss really was an asshole today. I had a good reason." Then comes the plan, "Tomorrow I promise I won't go to the doughnut shop, no matter what! I'll bring a healthy snack in the car so I won't need to. I can do this!" And with these last thoughts, the good feeling returns. Then what happens the next day or maybe two to three days later? You guessed it. We're back at the doughnut shop. And why is that? It's because the "I" voice in our heads is not connected to reality. The whole thing is nothing but a mental exercise to experience misery and then find peace again. We could even go so far as to call it mental masturbation if we don't mind being a little crass.

Now let's turn back to mental illness. The monster really isn't the scary or depressed thoughts themselves. The monster is the ongoing process of trying not to feel afraid or depressed; trying to figure out what you are really afraid of or what is making you sad; trying to numb the feelings, stop the thoughts, and trying to convince your "self" that you are no longer afraid or depressed.

The mind produces an idea that triggers a feeling response in our bodies. Then the mind produces the idea of a person (supposedly you) who doesn't like the feeling and the thoughts that made them feel that way. Then the mind comes up with ways to numb the fearful or depressed feelings. Then it might take on the persona of the wise, self-aware one who can figure out once and for all what you are really afraid of and how to not feel afraid anymore. My mind particularly loves this last projection. It can sound so smart, talking for hours about psychological theory and all my personal childhood traumas that might once and for all uncover the secret root of the fear that I feel. It believes that doing so will oncover the revelation that will once and for all make me never have to feel fear again—which is totally impossible, by the way. All the while, as I am immersed in this mental fantasy land and endless goose chase of nonexistent eternal peace and happiness, life in all of its complex brilliance and with all of its infinite opportunities, passes me by.

Do you know what the purpose of all this distraction originating from the mind is? It's two-fold. Pay very close attention now, because this is HUGELY important. It isn't to torture you—although it certainly does a good job of that. The purpose is to help you get a high from the thoughts that come at the end of the cycle AND to keep you small and safe. You see, your mind learned long ago that you are not enough and deeply flawed. So all the mind is really after is a small existence where you get occasional hits of feeling peaceful and happy. When all your energy and attention are going to this crazy tail-chasing thought circle, you don't have energy for real life. But if you believe deep down that you are insufficient or deeply flawed, that is actually a perfect place for your energy to go.

Once again, this is just an intelligent effort of life to keep you safe. Because someone who is truly broken must indeed stay small in order to survive. Someone who is broken and incapable should never take risks in the world or embark on adventures. To do so would be suicide. No, for the truly flawed and fucked-up person, navel-gazing really is the best option in order to stay safe and survive. The thing is, there is nothing wrong with you. There never was. You only came to believe that because of the teaching and treatment of the confused and probably abused people who took care of you when you were a child. So this navel-gazing and tail-chasing is completely nonsensical. It's time to wave goodbye to that crazy train and sink your teeth into real life. What the hell are you waiting for?

CHAPTER 20
WHEN IT PAYS TO BE MISERABLE

There's one other piece of this puzzle that is important to address before we talk about healing, and it goes back to understanding that there is an intelligent reason for all behavior. We have already talked about several intelligent reasons for maladaptive thought patterns. But there is a very important one that can be a huge fuel source to keep the fire of mental illness and exhausting tail-chase burning. The reason is this: many of us learned at an extremely deep level that misery is safe, and in many cases, even that misery is equivalent to love. I learned to associate low and sad feelings with safety at a very young age, to the point that it seemed incredibly risky and uncomfortable to consider being well. The intelligent being that you are will do anything to ensure that you are safe, and therefore, it will tirelessly run in circles of misery if misery is believed to be the way of safety and survival. In these cases, it seems well worth it to perpetually suffer. I will never forget one of the first times that I was confronted with this tendency in my own life. I mentioned previously that I dealt with a variety of health issues after the birth of my first child, and one of them was contracting a bacterial gut infection called Clostridium Difficile (c-diff) after taking a round of antibiotics. This particular type of infection can be quite serious, and it can also be very hard to get rid of. I can remember feeling so stressed about it, spending hours combing the internet in a haze of hopeless desperation, trying to find an alternative healing method that didn't involve just taking rounds of additional antibiotics (the typical suggested treatment). Even though my mind was saying that it wanted so badly to fix this problem, the truth was that wallowing in this kind of misery was very familiar and comfortable for me. Let me tell you what made me realize this. After working with a holistic health practitioner, I did another test to see if the bacteria still showed up in my system. I can remember when I received the phone call with the test results. The test came back negative; the bacteria was no longer present. I heard the news and hung up the phone, but I didn't feel anything—not excitement, joy, relief—nothing. Immediately after hanging up the phone, I walked into the kitchen and told my mother-in-law the good news. Her reaction was so enthusiastic and positive, and it was actually quite confronting because I realized that I didn't feel any of those things. I was truly more comfortable with the sadness, discomfort, and desperation. I couldn't admit it at the time, but I was able to see this years later.

There are so many ways that we can learn that misery is safe or that love feels like misery. People who grow up in homes that are largely unhappy automatically associate suffering with a safe state. In other words, it feels like "home."

Another influence that programs people to embrace endless suffering is the understanding that the world is inherently a very dark place. The religion that I grew up with was steeped in this understanding. We were taught that because of the "original sin" committed by Adam and Eve, darkness and evil entered the world and are the prominent forces in the material world until death and passage into heaven finally end the suffering. Aside from religion, this understanding can be very common if you grew up with caregivers who were depressed or deeply unhappy. Families with these kinds of caregivers will often assert their belief that the world is an unhappy place and will passionately defend that belief because it justifies their own experience.

If you grow up with this understanding, there is no incentive to look for new ways of seeing life and the world or for letting go of maladaptive thought patterns. You simply accept that this world and your experience in it are dark and uncomfortable and always will be, except for brief intermissions.

Taking this last misunderstanding one step further, some of us were taught that God punishes you if you feel too safe or happy. Think about some of the pithy little sayings that supposedly give wisdom and guidance, such as, "We plan, God laughs." I think this saying was originally supposed to suggest that life is unpredictable, but it has a certain malicious flavor to it if you ask me. The religion that I grew up with had a certain emphasis on our need to "depend" on God, which was rather extreme. God was almost portrayed as some sort of insecure meathead who needed his partner to be weak, dependent, and unskilled. People who were too confident or planned too much or relied too much on other things, like money or their health, were systematically knocked off their feet so that they would learn to be dependent on God. This view goes hand-in-hand with the sinfulness of the world and humanity and the need for people to be constantly self-examining and confessing their wrongdoing to God. Ultimately, in this thought camp, God rewards people who are lowly, dependent, low-functioning, and self-critical. So many maladaptive thought patterns might seem invaluable because they provide a direct pathway to receiving God's love and care. And once again, even if God and religion are not part of the picture, caregivers who are unhappy or depressed can actually feel threatened by emotions such as joy, excitement, confidence, or pride. In my family, we received a lot of well-intentioned care and affection if we were feeling depressed, inadequate, or lost. If we were feeling confident, proud, or enthusiastic, they didn't quite know what to do with us. So guess what? I expressed confusion, loss, and low feelings much of the time. It ensured attachment and love from the people who mattered most.

The last reason that it can seem like it "pays" to be miserable is for simple ego-protection reasons. It is vulnerable to hope for or try to achieve something better. Many of us avoid the vulnerable position of making true change in hopes of achieving a better state because we want to avoid the possibility of failure at all costs. Our old thought patterns and habits are so predictable and familiar. Moreover, the identity of being anxious, depressed, or a victim of any kind of mental illness gives much fuel to the version of me that lives in my head (the mental narrator who speaks in first person). If those problems were really solved, the self-image (the voice) in the mind would have nothing else to do.

Exactly.

In that case, the mind could fulfill its true role of imagination (for fun or practical purposes) instead of playing the desperate and futile role of pretending to be me—the role it's been playing for as long as I can remember.

CHAPTER 21
TURNING AWAY FROM THE TRUE IDENTITY

When a child is punished for authentic self-expression, they learn to fear their true self because it threatens their attachment, which they depend on to survive. Authentic emotion and expression become the enemy. They are something to be feared. Gabor Maté writes about this so eloquently in his book *the Myth of Normal: Trauma, Illness & Healing In A Toxic Culture*. He asserts that children have two core needs—(1)attachment and (2)authenticity. In his words:

Although both needs are essential, there is a pecking order: in the first phase of life, attachment unfailingly tops the bill. So when the two come into conflict in a child's life, the outcome is well-nigh predetermined. If the choice is between 'hiding my feelings, even from myself, and getting the basic care I need' and 'being myself and going without,' I'm going to pick that first option every single time. Thus our real selves are leveraged bit by bit in a tragic transaction where we secure our physical or emotional survival by relinquishing who we are and how we feel. (Maté, *the Myth of Normal*, pp. 107-108)

When we fear and deny our instinct or gut feelings, we turn our back on our true identity, which is connected to everything and responding in real time. We turn our back on the truth of our being. We turn our back on the flow of intelligence responding in the present. In turning away from truth, we turn toward the talking voice in our head, which is nothing more than an identity created by our brilliant imaginations from the fragments of our conditioning and experience, especially our traumatic experience. The voice in my head (and the voice in your head) is, at its core, a traumatized child trying to fit in and secure its survival.

We deny the truth of our being and submit to our conditioning. We do this because it seems like the only way to survive. And it's not working! When we walk around mesmerized by our personal narrator, whose every word is based on learned confusion and misunderstanding, we inadvertently mold our lives to fit its misconceptions. The result is most often suffering and a tremendous sense of being lost. The good news is that we do not have to stay there, and oddly enough, the disarray of the mind is the doorway to the path home.

PART 7:
AN UNLIKELY GUIDE – LET THE FUCKED-UP MIND SHOW YOU THE MAGIC OF WHO YOU ARE

CHAPTER 22
HEALING BY SEEING

"Until you make the unconscious conscious, it will direct your life, and you will call it fate."

- Carl Jung

At this point, there are several new points of understanding that we know are helping us to clear up the shit storm of confusion that we used to refer to as our "mental disorder." We know that the very core of any "mental disorder" is a subconscious belief of being flawed, insufficient, or unsupported. This belief originated from damaging teaching or interactions that we encountered when we were young. Regardless of the original intent of the teaching or interaction, our system interpreted it and stored it as a version of one of these beliefs: "There is something wrong with me"; "I am not enough"; "I am not supported in this world"; and even "God or the Universe is punishing me or out to get me."

This segues directly into the second concept, which is

this: The belief that we just talked about is charged with a molten mess of suppressed emotion—usually a combination of fear, rage, sadness, and shame. It has to generate this kind of emotion because all of these forms of belief literally go against the nature of life. They are the opposite of how life functions in its natural state (uninterrupted by wild stories of the human imagination). Life in its natural state is all about thriving. Every single living organism, without exception, is perfectly equipped to operate as it was designed with powerful instincts for survival. This can be seen in an organism as simple as the single-celled amoeba. Even as basic as they are, amoebas automatically move away from light that is too strong or temperatures that are too hot or too cold (Amoeba, n.d.). They are wired to survive. We, like the amoeba, are brilliantly equipped to thrive and survive. Not only this, but the environment is designed to support us in this. There is oxygen to breathe and food to eat. However, unlike the amoeba, we have the ability to believe that the opposite is true. That being said, one of the brilliant features of the human design is that when we have these faulty beliefs lodged in our system, we encounter uncomfortable feelings that let us know something is awry. So thank goodness that faulty beliefs are charged with intense, uncomfortable emotion. These feelings might arise in response to a specific trigger that directly activates the faulty belief, such as when your partner acts in a slightly dismissive way, and a tidal wave of rage and shame erupts through your body because of a deep belief that you are not important or worthy of love. In other cases, the feeling may arise spontaneously in the form of a panic attack that seems to bubble up out of nowhere. In this situation, it is very likely that the system of the person has reached a point where it seems best for the person to recognize or to be made aware of the faulty belief and the stress that it is causing to the system.

Many people are being confronted with these kinds of feelings and emotions, which is why mental illness diagnoses are so prevalent. Most of us have suppressed these emotions all our lives because we learned to run from discomfort in the real world. We learned that we need to shut these kinds of sensations out and/or numb them in order to function properly. Honestly, a lot of us were probably even taught that having intense experiences of these emotions means that we have some sort of irreparable genetic mood disorder, and that faulty teaching made us all the more desperate to get away from them.

This brings us to the third key concept, which is that our incredibly creative little minds have gone to work ever since then, attempting to use their imaginative powers to explain this closed box of intense emotions.

The specific variation of our mind's stories, albeit fearful or depressive, depends on the life experiences we have had. Regardless of the specific flavor of the stories, they are all an attempt of the mind to make sense of the feeling. We became confused by taking the stories literally (which sent us down a long and frustrating rabbit hole). However, we now know that the content of the mind's stories is irrelevant. The mind is simply trying to create a story to explain unprocessed emotions and false beliefs. Moreover, it is trying to create an illusion of responsibility and control in the mental world since we grew up believing that we were on our own and completely unsupported by the Universe in the real one.

We also know that "thinking more" is not the answer. We've turned away from our true nature and from the natural flow of action in reality and participated in a hypnotic and toxic relationship with the mind because we believed that it would help keep us safe and find our way home. We've done way too much of that already. It's time to break the addiction.

So now I want to tell you how your mind and body can be used to heal you and guide you home. When you think a thought that disturbs you and your body is engulfed in intense emotion, you are being given an opening to healing. This is also true even if no thought is present and intense emotions come up seemingly from nowhere. Let me tell you how. While the specific content of whatever thought that triggers the emotions is 1000 percent irrelevant (remember, it's just a made-up story), whatever story it is, happens to be lighting up or resonating with the frequency of your particular flavor of belief of "I am wrong or not ok in the world." When that button gets pushed and the emotion lights up, you are being given an opportunity to let the emotion be there by being present with it and letting it process naturally. This is what you used to do when you were a child, when you knew that you were whole and perfect and miraculous simply because of your sheer existence. Children know that they are whole and well, and therefore, they do not fear or suppress any emotion. They know that this life experience is about feeling, and so they do it with gusto. My daughters show me this every day. My 16-month-old jumps into my arms and wilts against me in fear when she hears the loud noise of the vacuum cleaner. My three-year-old turns beet red and swings her fists in rage when she feels she has been mistreated. My five-year-old literally bounces whenever she is happy or excited. My seven-year-old cries with all her might in the deepest sadness when she feels that one of her sisters is being mean to her. There is no holding back, no suppressing, no hesitancy. In all of these emotional experiences, there is complete and utter surrender to the experience, and then it passes, forgotten. And they truly are more resilient because of it.

So let's say that you are in your office on a work day, and you start to feel the familiar sensations of panic rising up and gathering in the pit of your stomach or inside of your throat. Or maybe you are playing with your small child, and an intrusive thought of harming them crosses your mind along with a surge of adrenaline and terror. Or maybe you wake up first thing in the morning only to be greeted by the heaviest feelings of sadness, exhaustion, and darkness that you could imagine. Instead of giving your attention to your mind and what it is saying, turn all of your attention to the feeling in your body. What is happening in that moment is not some psychological symptom that needs to be diagnosed, medicated, or exterminated. What is happening in that moment is that you are being given a small opening to come face-to-face with the harm and misunderstanding that you encountered and internalized as a child. You are being given a window into your inner programming, the code or screen of beliefs always operating below the level of consciousness that your inner intelligence is guided by. This opportunity is precious, and you don't want to waste it. So with everything you have, turn your attention to the feeling in your body. When you do this, you stop getting lost in the wild stories of the mind, and you begin giving your awareness or attention to the intense sensations that the mind is trying to explain. You hold the feelings of panic, terror, depression, and rage like a little toddler having the biggest tantrum of their life, and by holding them and giving them your loving attention—even while your mind is screaming that it hates doing it— you begin to heal and break free from the madness. You hold your experience in a way that nobody else was able to hold you as a child. And by doing this, you set yourself free. Even if your mind starts spouting what sounds like good advice or ideas about exactly what your particular "false belief" is, don't give your attention to the mind. Stay with the feeling. That is the only thing that is real, true, and certain. The coach and author Marnix Pauwels expressed this in a way that I love (translated from the Dutch original):

Stay with it a little longer.

Just a little longer than you think you dare.

Just a little more neutral than you're used to.

Just a little more curious than it seems.

Let the story about the feeling come and go.

Forget the idea that you need to understand what's playing.

Don't look for the meaning.

And stay pure to the physical sensation;

Just a little wider than your old boundaries.

Just a little closer than your safe distance.

Just a little longer than you thought possible.

Stay with it a little longer.

And behold: it solves itself again.

When the mind tells a story that hits your depression button, or your anxiety button, or your OCD button, and the body starts reacting, or if you start experiencing any of these reactions without the presence of conscious thought, you have been given an opportunity to heal. We have always attempted to stop the feeling while looking to the mind for guidance. This is the coping strategy that we learned when we were young, but it perpetuates a never-ending cycle. It affirms the false beliefs that we are broken or not equipped to handle reality. It also turns our attention away from our true self and wisdom and toward the mind and the imagined self that is made of fear and bad conditioning.

Then, before you know it, you are off to the races: An imagined self trying to solve imaginary problems in an imagined world. It is utter madness, but it feels like the only thing that makes sense. Instead, when your mind drops a bomb and/or your body lights up with intensity, staying in truth and reality means giving your attention to what is real. The only things that are real in this scenario are the feelings in your body and anything else that is happening around you. You sit with the feelings, and you let the mind rage on without buying into whatever it is saying. By doing this, you are standing in your true self with what is real, AND you are allowing your body to process the emotions attached to the false belief—which simultaneously disproves the belief. It disproves the belief (even if you do not know what the specific belief is) because when you stand firm and hold the experience of the feeling (without running away with the mind), you are affirming two truths with your actions:

3. You are whole and strong enough to hold whatever experience is there.
4. You are connected to the intelligence of life, and you trust that it supports you in every single moment.

By holding the emotion and the unnamed belief behind it in your presence, you are realigning yourself with what is true, what you knew by default when you were born. You are learning (remembering) that you are connected to a limitless source of wisdom, that you can handle reality, including intense feelings or even the darkest of feelings, and that the real you is never in your mind (imagination), but is responding in real time in this moment. When you really start to see the truth of this, the appearance of the thoughts, feelings, and emotions that we have run from for decades are seen for the powerful allies that they are. They might not feel good in the moment, but they are our keys to freedom, doorways out of the imagined vortex of the mind to living in reality.

You can only live your full potential in this life when you know from experience that you are big enough, strong enough, and brave enough to hold uncomfortable emotions—when you can give your attention to whatever emotion arises instead of letting it run to your mind with its explanations, problems, and solutions. When you achieve this, you free yourself from the lies of misunderstanding that you were taught as a child, and from the all-encompassing problems that your well-meaning imagination invented to protect you. And all of a sudden, your energy is free to act in pure intelligence in the world. This can look like solving world hunger or fully experiencing the company of the small child who is under your care. The possibilities are limitless.

It's also important to note that as we set out to take advantage of these healing opportunities, our minds will always try to convince us that their stories are indeed real and legitimate and that they require (yes, you guessed it) MORE THOUGHT! But this really can never be true. The stories are all variations of the deepest lie and confusion in the history of humanity. It is so important to understand that it is impossible that we are wrong, bad, or unsupported in this world. Just like the amoeba, every living thing is naturally equipped to live the life it is designed to live and instinctively does what makes sense in the moment based on what it can see.

You are no exception; you never have been. Now you are taking the lead in setting yourself free from the misery of that confusion. Not the little "you" in your imagination, but the real YOU that is part of the great intelligence that makes everything possible.

CHAPTER 23
TRUST THE LOVER THAT MOVES YOU

"The Intelligence of this physical system is unquantifiable. The human capacity for imagination and conceptualization, for ideas and thought, is equally limitless.
And when the two are understood for what they are, when the idea of a controlling self dies in the face of the unknowable intelligence of life that we really are, then the life we are is lived with the freedom, respect, and awe we deserve."

- Clare Dimond

So you see, your troubled mind and unruly physical symptoms are truly gifts. They are the way home to uncovering and healing deep misunderstandings in your subconscious programming. This alone is invaluable, but the fucked-up mind does something else as well. The frenzied and even nonsensical mind shows the *insignificance* of thoughts and reveals the truth: a force beyond the mind is living, breathing, and moving you. Let me tell you what I mean by giving you an example. One of my intrusive thoughts happens when I am driving my car, and my brain keeps playing the scenario of driving off the road or into oncoming traffic. While my brain colorfully paints this scenario and my body reacts with a light show of sensation, my body keeps safely driving the car down the road. Not only does it safely drive down the road, but at one point, a little squirrel runs out into the street, and before my mind has time to think, my body makes a calculated swerving motion to keep both the squirrel and me safe.

So who is doing the driving? Is it the "I" in my head that is busy playing a horror movie of self-destruction? It can't be. My body isn't taking any of the actions that are going through my mind. In fact, everything that my body is doing is happening without thought. The safe driving, the dodging of the squirrel—these things are happening automatically. How is that possible? It is possible for the same reason that the little amoeba automatically moves away from harsh light or temperature. It is because we are being lived by the very source of life itself. Me, you, the squirrel—we're all being lived by life, the thing that breathes for us and causes our cells to function and the Earth to spin on its axis. The greatest secret of life is that intelligence—the impulse to survive and to thrive—is the real, living you, and the "I" that speaks in your head absolutely is not. Now, if your mind had always behaved itself, it might actually be much harder to stumble across this truth. Our minds are so clever, and they do a masterful job of convincing us that they are in control and calling the shots. But when you are driving down the road and see yourself driving into oncoming traffic, and it doesn't happen, you're seeing the truth laid out in front of you on a silver platter. You are not your mind, and the "I" in your mind has no power to act. Not only is it powerless, but we might even say that it doesn't exist at all. It is a figment of your imagination.

You might take a moment to thank your fucked-up mind for the messenger of truth that it is. Without it, you might have lived your whole life in a confused illusion, running around fighting every new imaginary problem that your imagination spits out and fulfilling the small and rather pointless existence fitting of the shitty self-image that was handed to you. Thanks to your ill-mannered thoughts, you don't have to. You can be free.

I think we can safely say at this point that you are most definitely not the voice in your head. You don't choose what the voice says. More importantly, the content and opinions of the voice are continuously changing. One minute, it says one thing, and the next, it might say the complete opposite. Not only are you not the voice in your head, but the voice in your head is nothing more than a programmed narrator. It is an incredibly intelligent machine that has accumulated massive quantities of taught information over the course of your life. Some of this information has been useful, like knowing what country, state, and city you live in and having a stash of interesting facts to throw out in conversations at happy hours. However, it has likely absorbed a good deal of misinformation as well. Much of this misinformation has been compiled into the formation of an idea of who you are—a sort of avatar image of yourself that only exists in the world of thought. It is a seemingly concrete image with a fixed personality, fixed strengths, fixed weaknesses, and a fixed mental future.

That image or avatar is a creative masterpiece. Think about it for a second. The mind has created an entire character, one that could be the protagonist of a movie or the hero of a novel. Even more impressive is that the creation is so good that you believed that that character was real and that that character actively makes all of the decisions for your body. Your fate, your health, your success, and most importantly, your very survival are believed to be in the hands of this (often flawed) character. What is incredibly mind-blowing beyond belief is that the character is completely fictional. He or she never existed and never will. The character is a compilation of learned information aggregated over time. The character is nothing more than a creative masterpiece.

So if that character isn't living your daily life, then who is? Who are you, really? The best answer that I have found for this question is this: You are intelligence. Period. You are the intelligence of the Universe living in a human body and seeing the world through the screen of what you have learned over time. This intelligence that you are is constantly learning and adapting based on the information it receives.

Consider this for a moment. When you came into the world as a tiny baby, the image of yourself that you have today had never even been thought of. It didn't exist. In spite of this, your body functioned beautifully. You cried when you were hungry. You fell asleep when you were tired. You gradually achieved developmental milestone after developmental milestone, such as reaching out for toys, crawling, sitting, and walking. And the intelligence that you are did all of these things without any concept of self. You did these things because the intelligence that you are couldn't help but do them. You, just like every other living thing in the Universe, are a living force that is naturally wired to grow, flourish, and thrive. You automatically do whatever makes sense for that purpose (for the sake of survival) without thinking. You are still the life that moved the body of the intelligent little baby that you once were. You just acquired a lot of beliefs along the way compiled into your personal avatar image, and you, like the rest of us, fell for the great illusion that comes with having a brilliant human mind—that you are an isolated little self, left to fend for itself and independently come up with a way to survive in the world.

Every thought, every idea, every suggestion is automatically evaluated by the intelligence that you are. Action follows this evaluation, and all of this happens below the level of the conscious mind. The mind might talk as if it is making the choices, but it is only an imagined voiceover. Let me give you one more example to illustrate this, because it can be difficult to grasp after a lifetime of believing that the mind is choosing the choices that we make. I can remember when I was deep in the throes of panic and terrifying, intrusive thoughts. My mind was always coming up with "Christian" ways to deal with this "problem" because that is how I was raised. Although I was raised by highly conservative and orderly Christians who didn't participate in things like healings and casting out demons, my in-laws practiced Latin American Christianity, which was all about the healings and more woo-woo Christian practices, and I was exposed to this possibility through them. So when I was really suffering with thoughts and feelings that seemed so "bad," my mind would fixate on these types of potential "fixes" as something that I should explore, something that maybe would finally set me free and prevent bad things from happening. So I would witness my mind think about it and think about it, and it would cause a lot of stress and additional misery. Then one day, I had a realization that even though my mind was fixating on the possibility of seeking out some sort of religious healer, there wasn't an ounce of energy in my body that was going to act on these thoughts. Why? Because deep down, I didn't believe that it was the answer. My mind could continue screaming at me until the end of time about how I should go find a church where spiritual healing is practiced and walk to the front and ask to be healed, and my legs would never put forth the effort to stand up and do it because the intelligence that is living me simply doesn't believe it. Intelligence moves the body—not the mind.

How is all this relevant to the topic of mental illness? Well, quite honestly, it is everything. The content of fucked-up thoughts can vary beyond what we can measure. After all, they are inventions of the human imagination, which is truly limitless. Dark thoughts of depression, racing thoughts of panic, repetitive thoughts of checking and reassurance, or wild, intrusive thoughts involving shame or destruction are common productions of minds that have inherited lies and confusion. These images arise in thought, and because the role of your mind or imagination is to make the unreal appear real in your awareness, the image plays out in full color with flawless special effects, and therefore, your body reacts accordingly with sensations of fear or sadness. It can appear so real that it even feels like the scene is happening. But it is never more than a vivid image in your mind and a wave of physiological and emotional responses in your body.

The intensity of such thoughts and the body's reactions, combined with a misunderstanding of the mind and forgetting our true nature, can trap people in prolonged misery. They mistakenly believe that they are the voice in their head and are, therefore, crazy or deeply flawed. They might take medications that are addictive or have bad side effects. They might constrict their lives and avoid people and situations that are related to their fearful thoughts. They might lie in bed day after day because they hear depressed thoughts saying that they are worthless and incapable, and the feelings that accompany those thoughts make the content of the thoughts seem true. They might spend years in psychotherapy and live with a continuous obsession for fixing themselves and making their unwanted thoughts disappear. They might (like my grandfather) constrict their lives to such an extent and get so lost in their convoluted thought world that they take their own life, because that seems like the most loving and merciful outcome in the context of their incredible suffering and feelings of lostness (and isolation from truth). All these outcomes, in their varying degrees of severity, are the result of someone unnecessarily living as a prisoner of their brilliant imagination.

Freedom comes from seeing that you are nothing more than intelligence in continuous motion. Nothing, not even the highest quantity of learned, shitty beliefs, can change that. You are the intelligence of the Universe. And let's return to the subject of intrusive thoughts for a moment because they are a part of every mental illness, and they have a special place in my heart. Intrusive thoughts will always be powerless because they don't make sense to the intelligence that you are. The funny thing is that if you are a person who experiences "intrusive thoughts," you can actually be 100 percent sure that you will never act on them, even more than the average person. You have identified them as intrusive thoughts because they don't align with your values, and they do not make sense to you. Therefore, the intelligence that you are will never put them into motion. Period. The intelligence that you are might take measures to avoid the possibility of acting on them if you've never truly seen that they are harmless. But that is just another act of intelligence for a system with limited knowledge. You are always intelligence in action.

CHAPTER 24
DON'T LIVE IN THE PAST

A while back, I listened to a podcast episode from Dr. Amy Johnson called, "How You're Living in the Past, and Not Realizing It." It offered insight into some of the sneaky ways that we fall back into the same old misunderstanding, causing us to run in circles for a while.

What does it mean to live in the past? We might picture someone who refuses to let go of an old conflict or argument and who repeatedly brings it up and makes decisions because of its implications. We might also envision someone who experienced some sort of failure in the past and who can't seem to get over it. Instead, they seem to wallow in it and talk about it incessantly when everyone around them can see that if they would only forget about it and move on, they could accomplish a lot and have great success in life. Those are some of the immediate examples that come to mind.

However, there is a whole other level of living in the past that we all do on a daily basis. In fact, this kind of living in the past is hard-wired into our cultural understanding and language. It's a part of our daily conversations, our decisions, and is even integral to our very understanding of who we are.

In the podcast episode that I listened to, Dr. Johnson talked about how every single thought that we have, regardless of the content, is somehow a reflection of the past. This is true in so many different capacities. First off, the very thoughts that come into your mind are a reflection of learned behavior, perspectives, and language. We've talked about that a lot already. Everything that you think has been learned at some point in the past. Let's go a step further. Whenever you think a thought, even if it seems like you are thinking about what is currently happening, the thought has to be about the past, even if it happened half a second ago (as the podcast points out). If you're thinking about it, it has already happened, period.

Now wait a second (you might be thinking), what about when I'm thinking about the future? Good point. Except that every time you think about what might happen in the future, the image that is portrayed is either based on past experience, past thoughts, or past learnings. It certainly isn't based on reality, so it has to be from one of those things. For example, when I used to be a business consultant before going back to school for my master's degree, I would always get extremely anxious if I had to do any sort of public presentation. My mind would play different embarrassing scenarios where I would be giving the presentation and then spontaneously go blank, so that I was left standing mute in front of the audience. These thoughts were not based on past experience, but they were based in past learnings because they most likely originated from some sort of movie, television show, or "funny" story that I had heard about someone who gave a public presentation. Because of this, they had nothing to do with the future and everything to do with the past.

So yes, literally everything that we think is about the past. Why should you care about this? Because if you don't know this at a deep level, then you will always live in the past, and you will completely miss what is real. Let's start with an example that is really popular in the current cultural jargon: personality types and traits. Myers-Briggs, The Enneagram, Typefinder, Big Five Assessment, and astrology are just a few methods of analysis, and the list goes on and on. But even if taking personality assessments and looking at the stars are not your thing, you probably have a memorized list of traits that you ascribe to yourself that automatically gets rattled off any time someone asks you what you are like. "I love parties." "I hate crowds." "I'm terrible at public speaking." "I'm an introvert." These are just a few examples of the countless ways that people describe themselves on a daily basis. These kinds of assertions take up a large part of the average contemporary interpersonal conversation.

Honestly, I think our minds like this kind of categorization so much because they appear to make us, and consequently, life, feel more solid and predictable. If I will always like the same things, dislike the same things, want the same things, and act the same way, it makes life highly predictable, manageable, and controllable. You know the problem with this? It is utterly and completely untrue, a total illusion. But our minds are thrilled with the concept, and so they get really good at focusing on and remembering the times when our personalities appear consistent. They are also really good at ignoring or outright dismissing any evidence that contradicts the trend.

It's also important to point out that we become attached to certain character traits that we ascribe to ourselves, even seemingly negative or undesirable ones. Try to show someone who claims that they are a "really anxious person" evidence that they are not always anxious. Nine times out of ten, they will argue with you until they are blue in the face. Is this because they like being anxious? Of course not. But somewhere along the line, they learned that being an "anxious person" is an integral part of their life experience. To them, it looks like an irreplaceable component of who they are. Life just wouldn't make sense without it.

At this point, you might be thinking, "Wait a minute, I DO notice certain behaviors or traits or qualities that repeat themselves in my experience over and over again." And to that I would say, "Of course you do." The life that animates our bodies is always learning and acquiring new ways of being and doing in the world that it deems to be most advantageous for our survival. So it can and does repeat the same behaviors. Think about a professional athlete who seems to magically execute the same muscle movements over and over again. I used to wonder how professional athletes are not always ridden with anxiety that they might begin their next game or competition and completely fail to perform. I wondered this because I didn't understand how life works. The professional athlete is being lived by intelligence that remembers and builds on learned skills and survival techniques. You and I are being driven by the same intelligence, which is why we also repeat certain behaviors and tendencies—because in a previous point in our lives, they seemed to help us or work for us in some capacity. Just like the professional athlete doesn't spontaneously lose skills and ability, we don't forget our behavioral habits UNTIL we realize at a deep level that there is a better way that we can act. Intelligence is also always learning, and will change behavior when it makes sense to do so. So in that very real sense, there is absolutely no such thing as a fixed personality. However, when we believe that there is such a thing, and we make decisions based upon that understanding, our lives are navigated based upon false information. We live in the past.

Not only do we do this with ourselves, but also with the people around us. I just looked across the table at my husband and realized this for myself all over again. When I look at him, I see his handsome Latino face with dark black hair. He's got his favorite notebook open and is making notes about financial realities and possibilities and what it means for the future (one of his favorite pastimes). He looks up with a smile and says, "What is the Katheriné (pronounced intentionally with an exaggerated Latino accent) doing?" My mind wants to be able to put my husband in a box. He's the funny one. He's the mathematical one. He's good at this and bad at that. If I say this, I know he'll respond this way. But just like me, he is life constantly learning and adapting. And although he, like me, has repeated certain behaviors and traits in the past, really, anything is possible and always will be. Can you even imagine how out of control we really are? It's mind-blowing! But in addition to how out of control we are, can you imagine how much potential we have? Anything is possible.

The other amazing thing is that when the truth of this adaptability sinks in, we can have whatever "personality" makes sense and even have fun with it. You are not confined to any fixed personality; you can adopt any role in life that aligns with the intelligence guiding you and makes sense in the moment. Your personality could completely transform in the next moment because the traits that you've developed and held onto for years simply don't make sense anymore. For example, I used to be a completely stereotypical "people-pleaser." I couldn't bear the thought of upsetting people or causing conflict in any way. However, as I've learned and gained understanding, that way of being in the world simply doesn't make sense anymore. The behavior that flows out of me (often effortlessly) doesn't seek to make other people happy most of the time because it simply doesn't make sense to live that way. The intelligence that I am dropped a learned behavior and adopted a better one.

Personality is one area where we live in the past. We also live in the past when we carry around our mental list of personal "problems." I'm talking about our addictions, our depression, our anxiety, our rage issues, our OCD, and other mental health "disorders". To even say, "I have xyz disorder" is, by definition, living in the past. When we identify with a past experience or behavior, which is always the case when we label ourselves with any one of these or other problems, we are literally looking at something that happened in one moment or several moments in time because it made sense then, and taking it on as a permanent character trait.

Let me give you a silly example to show you what I am talking about. Let's say I walked out onto the street in front of my house to take a stroll. Out of the blue, a snake slithers out in front of me, and I instinctively jump over the thing to avoid stepping on it. All of this is logical behavior, and it makes sense in the moment. However, what if, after that experience, I went around describing myself to other people (and believing) that I am a person who "jumps in the street." A friend might suggest that you go for a hike in the woods with them, and you respond, "Oh, sorry. I cannot do that. I am a person who jumps in the street." Then you get an urge to just go lie down in the grass in your front yard to enjoy listening to the birds. However, you stop in your tracks because you remember, "I am a person who jumps in the street." How crazy is this?!?! And yet that is what we do. We drink alcohol because we have learned that we cannot handle uncomfortable feelings. We even do it over and over again because we have not yet learned that enduring the uncomfortable feelings is an option. And then we go around saying, "I am an alcoholic. I have a drinking problem." The truth is that for someone to overcome a drinking problem, they must recognize that the behavior no longer makes sense due to the harm it causes and understand their ability to endure uncomfortable feelings. It is also important to add that it makes no difference if these things are understood at an intellectual level. This is why the repetitive action of trying to think yourself out of damaging behaviors never works, because once again, the mind has no control over what you do. No, the understanding has to take place deep in the intelligence of your being, and this can happen in any number of ways.

The same is true for any maladaptive thought or mood problem that one can have. Let's consider a person who struggles with depression. This person experiences chronic low energy, brutal self-criticism, and a dismal view of themselves and all of life. Everyone tells them it is a chemical imbalance or hereditary. However, the more likely (and simpler) explanation is that this person grew up in conditions where these "symptoms" served a valuable purpose. Maybe their caregivers gave them love and attention only when they were sad. Maybe there were activities or experiences that the person was only able to avoid by being "ill." Maybe they had a single or repeated experience of being cruelly criticized, and they internalized it as a deep subconscious belief. Maybe the free expression of feelings was punished in their childhood home, and so they learned to stuff and silence feeling to avoid the external consequences. Maybe they experienced trauma that was so overwhelming and painful for a small child, and their intelligent system suppressed the feelings as a protective mechanism. Somehow, the "depressive" thoughts and feelings this person experiences served a purpose at some time. It has to be that way because our systems are intelligent. If they are wired to intelligently heal cuts and scrapes or even bones, how could it be different with the psyche and emotions? I am convinced that every psychological symptom begins as an intelligent attempt to keep the person safe and help them be whole.

However, the problems arise because the person looks to the mind as a trustworthy guide in an attempt to feel safe. The personal narrator in the mind, which is made of the belief that "there is something wrong with me," begins to focus on the experience of mental illness as part of the person's "problem." The mental narrator repeatedly talks about its dislike of the disorder and obsesses about how to "fix" the disorder. This mental narrative and pursuit takes on a life of its own. All of a sudden, the natural process of self-preservation is derailed. The person attaches to a *temporary* experience that was trying to improve their lives or at least to keep them safe, erroneously believing that the very thing that was trying to save them is some sort of new problem that needs fixing! This last sentence could be a synopsis of the conventional understanding and treatment of mental illness in our time. The intelligent response of the mind and emotions, along with the misguided explanation of the mind, are labeled with a diagnosis and treated as a disease. We have forgotten the intelligent origin of all of it, and as a result, many of us feel lost.

It's also important to point out that the mind is so incredibly good at bringing up the past in a manner that appears extremely wise and beneficial. Let me give you an example. The other day, I was leaving my bedroom, and I noticed that my husband's new workout shirt was hanging on the top edge of the clothes hamper. Something about it caught my eye. I focused on it, and I noticed that at the bottom hem on the inside of the shirt, the phrase "Better each day" was written. Immediately, my mind started babbling, "Oh yeah, that's exactly the mindset you need to have. You know, all these frustrations, the intrusive thoughts, the dark moods, all of it—you just need to focus on the fact that every day is a little better." Do you see how clever this is? Out of nowhere, the mind is acting as some sort of positive thinking coach. What is really happening, however, is a clever projection and reminder of the self-image, all of the associations of the past—the "problem." It's as if the mind is saying, "Now, don't forget your problem. THIS is who you are. Yeah, you might just be in your peaceful bedroom calmly going about your business without a real problem in the world, but don't forget that YOU are a person who deals with dark moods and scary thoughts. Never ever forget that." Because if you forget your problems, then there is nothing for the idea of you that lives in your mind to save you from. Really, there is no need for the "I" in your mind at all. And that, my friends, is the truth.

Watch out for these seemingly well-intentioned pep talks from the mind. Once you start to pay attention, you'll notice that they, just like the terrifying images or dark and condemning thoughts, are all doing the same thing. They are an attempt to draw your attention back to the past and to the carefully curated idea of the individual that you appear to be. There's nothing wrong with it. Never waste your energy trying to stop it. It's just what the mind does, and it makes life unbelievably interesting. Just notice it. That's what makes all the difference.

The personalities that we believe ourselves to have, as well as the problems (especially psychological problems), are both examples of "living in the past." There is another area where we constantly live according to our conditioning and experiences. This happens when we believe and live according to the commentary in our minds that is related to the present moment. I have four small children, and right now my full-time job is taking care of them, day and night. Because my children are small, there are plenty of moments when my home is full of loud noises. Sometimes it's screaming and shouting because the three-year-old and five-year-old are fighting over the same toy. Sometimes it's shrieking and sobbing because my highly active three-year-old tripped and bumped herself, again. Sometimes it's cries of excitement and sheer joy because they are having so much fun in their pretend play.

During any one of these scenarios, my mental narrator will often slip into a monologue of the frustrated victim. "I'm so tired of all the screaming and of the nonstop demands. I really need a break. I didn't get enough sleep last night. They shouldn't be acting like this. They should know better." The narrative and the feelings that accompany it are so familiar. The story is so believable. But it is nothing but a script from past learning and conditioning. How do I know this? Because really small children are excited and enthralled by any task, any experience, any responsibility. The *idea* that certain things are burdens or that certain behaviors and experiences shouldn't be happening is learned. The *idea* of not getting enough sleep to function is learned. The *idea* that I need time for myself when I don't feel good is learned. None of these ideas are true. The only thing that is true in any of these moments is what is actually happening in real time and the sensations that arise in the body. When you start to see this, everything changes.

Let me show you how. This morning, when I was frying an egg for my daughter and a fight broke out in the playroom, along with the realization that my two-year-old had pooped and needed a diaper change, the narrative started firing on all cylinders. "This is too much. I shouldn't have to deal with all of this. I'm going to lose it with these children." SO FAMILIAR. SO BELIEVABLE. It's like one of those nightmares where I signed up for a class in college and then never attended, and I just found out that I failed the semester. SO FAMILIAR. SO BELIEVABLE. But crazy enough, the mental narrative about my kids and the nightmare about failing the semester are equally true.

When I remember this, it frees my attention to notice what is true. I look out of my eyes, and I see my hand expertly grasping the spatula and flipping the egg to the other side to achieve the perfectly cooked over-easy egg that I'm famous for. I feel a hot sensation in my body and my heartbeat speeding up, calling my body to take action. That is the "this" of this moment. You might hear spiritual writers and teachers talk about "only this." Only this is real. Intelligence moving the limbs of the body. Intelligence moving the limbs of other little bodies. Smells. Feelings. Mental gibberish. This. When my attention focuses on and believes just this, my body is free to respond in a cleaner, simpler, softer way. There might even be space to experience the beauty and wonder and magic of this single moment of completely inexplicable existence.

When my attention is focused on the mental story, which is almost always made of past conditioning and pain, the moment is tainted with strain and resistance, and the magic is lost in a web of conditioned ideas. The more we realize this and repeatedly redirect our attention to reality as a new habit, the more we get to experience the magic. Who doesn't want magic? We've been after it ever since we were young.

CHAPTER 25
WHERE IS YOUR ENERGY GOING?

Have you ever watched a child play? I'm sure you have. But have you watched a child play recently? If you have, you probably noticed the uncanny quantity of energy that often flows through children. My kids do not stop moving. They're twisting, twirling, tasting, experimenting, dancing, jumping, rolling all day long from the minute they leap from bed in the morning until their heads hit their pillows at night. It's even become part of the understood cultural conversation about kids in this generation. I often hear adults say, "We have GOT to get to a park so these kids can burn off some of their energy!" or another classic, "Oh man, what I wouldn't give to have just a fraction of my kids' energy." Well, let me tell you a theory that I have. I truly believe that adults don't have any less energy than children. I believe that children's energy is flowing almost 100 percent toward living life rather than into thinking.

Look around at the average adults that you know.

Something that I have started to notice is how often, if you watch other adults, they clearly drift off into their thought-created world rather than being present with what is actually going on. Often, adults can be found staring off into the distance with a blank or slightly concerned look on their faces. They are disconnected from reality, lost in a world of unsolvable, non-existent problems that seem completely real and important to them. These people often appear to have very low energy. They are sluggish and dull, unmotivated and uninterested a large portion of the time. Is it because they intrinsically have less energy? No! It's because all of the energy that they have is flowing into the world of thought.

Think about it for a minute. All of that precious life-giving energy is pouring into the blabbering voice of an idea of a person that doesn't even exist. In other words, it is wasted. I cannot say this enough. This is why people who claim to suffer from depression, anxiety, OCD, and other mental disorders often appear to be so lifeless. It's because all of their energy is flowing away from life and into imagination. It makes so much sense!

Let's circle back to the title of this chapter. Where is YOUR energy flowing? Is it flowing into life, into reality? Are you engaged with the people in your life? Are you using your gifts and talents or developing new ones? Are you taking on challenges or at least participating in activities that you enjoy? I took a course recently with the brilliant Clare Dimond, and I saw for the very first time how precious and valuable our wants or desires are. They give us a channel into reality. They give direction to specific areas where we can truly engage with reality.

What is it that you want? What do you really want? To write a book? To have lunch with a specific someone? To take a ballroom dance class? To visit Malaysia? To learn to speak French? Then get off your ass and go for it! Get into the world. Get your hands dirty. Embarrass yourself. Get rejected. Be successful. Whatever. Just be in reality.

Keep in mind that as you start to shift your energy back toward life and away from being engaged in thought, you might experience two things. First, you might feel uncomfortable with the energy that you experience. I once heard Adyashanti say something like, "When you've spent most of your life dead, coming alive feels like dying." If you've spent the majority of your life completely lost in a complicated web of thought, it might have felt miserable, but that state almost definitely has become comfortably familiar. So, as your attention begins to turn away from the never-ending monologue of the thinking mind, the energy that you become aware of might feel extremely uncomfortable, even like it might be unbearable (even though it never is).

Quite honestly, I think that the energy that used to be

so invested in thought starts to rise and look for somewhere to go. Personally, I have experienced a lot of different, uncomfortable sensations in this process. One that has been a frequent experience is a sort of intense burning, tingling sensation in my face and chest. For years, I lumped it in with anxiety. However, when you peel away the mind's explanations and the labels that the mind has attached, all it is is energy.

So do this. Notice the labels. Notice the explanations. Your brain might automatically label the sensations of energy as anxiety (like mine) or even as a sign of some sort of physical problem, like high blood pressure or poor circulation. Then notice that in reality, all that is happening is rushes of energy. That's it. You are feeling and experiencing rushes of energy. What in the world is wrong with that? Isn't that actually a good thing? YOU HAVE ENERGY. Thank God! So use it. Find a place to direct this precious, magical resource. You might turn on some music and dance, or start writing that book you've dreamed of writing, or pick up a paintbrush for the first time in years, or go volunteer at the local animal shelter. The possibilities are infinite, and there is no wrong answer.

While we are on this topic of energy, it's important to recall a concept that we discussed earlier in this book. Do you remember why we started running to the mind in the first place? It was because we learned that our natural instincts and responses in the real world were not good enough or that the world was not safe. Because of this belief(s), many aspects of our experience, such as our emotions and even the feeling of tingling energy, can also feel dangerous and out of control. This is why our minds learn to pathologize them. However, rushing and pulsating energy is a precious gift. When you are living life, especially in relation to the things that are most important to you, you naturally experience rushes of energy. Does any part of that sound like a problem to you? To me, it sounds like a really positive thing. I want to experience rushes of energy when I am with my kids, spending time with my partner, doing my job, or starting a new business venture. Hell, even if I am just sitting on my couch doing nothing, I want to have rushes of energy. It means that I am alive and ready to participate in the world.

Let's go a step further. What if the rushes of energy that you experience are the EXACT SAME rushes of energy that a child experiences that inspire their little bodies to constantly fly into action? You experience a rush of energy and then, because you were conditioned to fear life, a troubling thought (anxious, intrusive, depressed, etc.) comes to mind, and your energy dives into the world of thought. A child experiences the same exact sensation, bursts into a silly twirling dance, and falls on the ground in a fit of laughter. Isn't that wild? Doesn't it make so much sense?

And why do you have intrusive thoughts and dive into convoluted thought webs instead of doing a somersault? Because somewhere along the line, you learned that you were not okay. When you believe that you are not okay, you experience out-of-control feelings, like intense rushes of energy, as a threat rather than a natural part of life, and even a gift. And then, when rushes of energy feel like a threat, the mind feverishly goes to work in its innocent ignorance, promising safety and a resting place, when all it is actually doing is running in circles around imaginary problems.

Seeing this is freedom, my friends. If I could reach through the pages or the screen and take you by the shoulders and shake you, I would. THIS IS FREEDOM. So take that rush of energy and run with it, no matter what your mind says. Take your fucking beautiful life by the horns and live it, in all of its gorgeous ups and downs and infinite variety. And then, if you forget to do this for a minute, or a day, or even a few months, just start again when you remember. Your life is already transformed just by reading this. It will never be the same again.

CHAPTER 26
AFRAID OF MYSELF

When we suffer from any sort of mental illness, we believe that we are afraid of any number of things. The depressed person fears the dark, low thoughts and feelings that plague them. The anxious person fears endless imaginary outcomes as well as the experience of a panic attack. The person with OCD fears repetitive loops of the mind and the paralysis that accompanies them. The person with intrusive thoughts fears their thoughts and the imagined possibility of them happening.

In truth, all of these people are deeply convinced that they are inadequate and that something is wrong with them. They have grown to fear their imaginations' creative inventions, attempting to express this paralyzing belief. Let's pause for just a moment to really appreciate what is happening here. Most of us live our lives convinced that we are a tiny, independently-deciding little person trying to navigate an enormous and very dangerous world, AND that we have the handicap of being deeply flawed and inadequate. How horrible is that?! This is the stuff of nightmares! And yet it is how most of us live our lives.

Children come into life completely unburdened by faulty beliefs and insecurities. They are pure life in motion, pure wisdom, really. Their energy is endless, their communication is unfiltered, and their exploration and creativity are boundless. They are pure authenticity, pure confidence, and pure intelligence acting in real time. The tragic thing that happens over and over again, however, is that when one of these perfect children is born to parents who are heavily conditioned and burdened by countless faulty beliefs and insecurities, the untamed, authentic, confident little creatures that enter their homes become highly confronting and even threatening. For an adult who has been living out beliefs such as –

- Life is hard.
- Other people are out to get me.
- The world is not safe.
- I always get the short end of the stick.
- I stay small and quiet so that I don't get noticed and abused.

– the natural behavior of a child will directly contradict these beliefs. If the caregiver is unwilling or unable to be curious about or question the way that they see the world, then the child's behavior is a massive threat to the stable foundation of their belief system. So what does that caregiver do? They often lash out at the child for anything that is confronting. Boundless energy is labeled as obnoxious, compulsive, or even as a disability. Innocent authenticity is labeled as rudeness. Their curiosity and questions are labeled as annoying. Their creativity and imaginations are labeled as silly or even dumb. Their confidence and bold exploration are labeled as dangerous. Their unfiltered feelings are labeled as wrong or bad. And depending on the home and the caregiver, these labels are coupled with all kinds of rules and punishments.

When we are trained as children that we should only feel certain feelings, we naturally start to monitor and fear our internal experience. Similarly, when we are repeatedly given feedback that our actions are bad or wrong or not good enough, we start to become fearful or apprehensive of our natural inclinations, and so we filter them through a thick screen of mental analysis and strategy.

That is how the unburdened, wild, and free embodiment of infinite life and intelligence in human form becomes a weighed-down, fearful, guarded, and insecure person. Here we are, perilously trying to fight our way through life, and the thing that we fear the most is ourSELF! We believe that there are monsters lurking all around us and that we are a problem to be managed. Surrounded by threats within and without, we believe our only saving grace to be the logical mind. So we give all our attention to the mind, a fearful imagination, believing that it will keep us safe and prevent us from suffering.

But the truth is that the logical mind and the narrating "I" voice inside are made of misunderstanding, and so by living in submission to the mind, we live out the same sad story over and over again. We run in circles of inadequacy and star as the protagonist who is broken and needs to be fixed in a never-ending saga.

The narrating mind and the self-concept formed when we learned that we were not enough. The mind knows no other story. So we trust a fearful imagination to lead us to the truth, and one wild story gets connected to another wild story, and before you know it, you're lost in a wildly convoluted wonderland of imaginary problems that seem very real and important, but that are simply imaginative reiterations of the belief that "I am not okay."

Let me give you an example from my own experience to show you what I mean. I've already referenced the time after my first daughter was born. It was by far the most difficult time in my life because of the intricate web of fears invented by my imagination. Just a few weeks after my daughter's birth, I thought I heard her cry and realized that the sound of my bedroom fan was similar to the sound of her distant cry. I remembered that my grandfather had started exhibiting symptoms of schizophrenia after the birth of his children, and my mind started to talk fearfully about the possibility of me "hearing things" that are not real and ending up like him. Then, when I started to deal with severe insomnia, those thoughts came up again, and my mind made a connection—what if the extreme lack of sleep would be the last straw to push me into a delusional state? The fear grew. During this time, I was a part of a Christian self-help group that was very progressive in terms of using nervous system calming techniques like tapping, alternate-nostril breathing, and even energy healing. However, the group had a big focus on a principle they referred to as "being mindful of your limitations." It referred to the idea that one should be humble enough to listen to limitations such as the body being tired, financial restraints, lack of time, illness, etc., and act accordingly. It's a very good principle, really. But there happened to be a lot of people with chronic illness in the group, so there was often a focus on rest and not doing "too much." Well, my mind started to focus on this in a very obsessive-compulsive way, fearing that if I did "too much," it could also somehow tip me over the stress threshold and into schizophrenia. There was also a hint of punitive religiosity to this last thought strand, almost as if I feared that God would smite me with mental illness if I wasn't "humble" enough to accept my limitations. This is when I was afraid of taking showers, as I mentioned earlier in the book. Do you see how lots of connections were made between unrelated things? Finally, when I started to experience intrusive thoughts and panic about harming myself or my daughter, my mind again connected this to the possibility of psychosis. Because I took my mind so seriously, these random fearful thoughts kept getting connected with new fearful thoughts, and before I knew it, I felt like I was literally walking on a tight rope over a huge pit of calamity. For the longest time, I couldn't see that every inch of the pit was created by my imagination. It all began with a very tired new mom who was really on edge and hyper-alert regarding her baby's needs. My deep belief that I was flawed and unsupported in the world was firing on all cylinders with this new challenge of motherhood, and my mind was trying to project this subconscious belief so that I could be aware of it and let go of its terrible weight.

This is our one true fear—that we are broken or not "okay". Because of this, we are afraid of untamed feelings and of natural inclinations and behaviors. We are afraid of ourselves. But there is a saving grace, and it is not the thinking mind. The saving grace for all of us is that we are all being lived, breathed, and moved by intelligence, and that intelligence knows deep down that it is enough, that it is connected to incredible wisdom, that it is an expert in surviving and thriving. Deep down, we still know this. That is why we keep fighting and searching to make ourselves okay. Because deep down, we know that we are. The more we align our awareness with the intelligent life that we are (that is always acting right now in real time), the more we remember this truth, and the more the confusion can fall away. We do this by giving our attention to the now instead of to the mind.

Healing is nothing more than remembering. You practice turning your attention away from the familiar and convincing mind and stay in the present moment, observing the magic of life living you right now. For me, this began with noticing small but powerful signals that a source of wisdom bigger than my mind was moving my body. I can remember a time when I was at the height of my terror of intrusive thoughts about harming my daughter, and she and I were upstairs together in her playroom. I was sitting on a couch, and she was running and tumbling next to me. She was probably about two years old. She was standing with her back against the couch and then, without warning, hurled herself backward so that she was falling headfirst toward the floor. Faster than I could think, I lurched forward and grabbed her foot with my hand, saving her from the collision with the floor. In that moment, I saw that something other than my mental voice was causing my body to move. Later, I was able to see this in an even more powerful way through the fact that, in spite of my extreme terror and panic, I never gave up on being a mom. Even though my mind was screaming at me that I was dangerous, that I was unfit, that maybe the loving thing to do was to take a step back and ask a family member to take more of a lead role in raising her, I never did. Do you want to know why? My mind accused me of just being proud and selfish, but really, it was because deep down, below the roaring of my mind, I knew the truth. I knew that I was a great mom and that there was nothing more important in the world than taking care of my daughter. Thankfully, I had also been exposed to enough psychological training to be able to question my mind a little bit (thanks to that progressive Christian self-help group that I was a part of), and I believe that helped as well. So I dug my heels in, and I stayed. Not only did I stay, but I had more children—because that is what I wanted in the intelligence of my being.

Limbs being moved. Words being said. Problems being solved. It's all inexplicable magic, really. And slowly, you start to remember. Slowly, the old stories don't make sense. They fall away because reality proves them to be wrong. This was the case when I started seeing that I was taking excellent care of my daughter and going above and beyond to ensure her well-being by waking up at all hours of the night with her, trying to feed her healthy food, comforting her whenever she was upset, and in many other ways while my mind was hurling denigrating accusations at me without stopping for breath. Healing is nothing more than remembering that we and everything around us are animated by magic. Even when the behavior appears sub-optimal, we are being lived by a source of wisdom and intelligence that the mind cannot fathom.

CHAPTER 27
THE NIGHTMARE THAT WAKES YOU UP

So how does one cross the bridge from living the tortured existence of a tiny, inadequate, broken individual fighting his or her way through a hostile and dangerous world to resting in inexplicable magic? The answer is through your fucked-up mind.

Really?

Yes. Really.

Fucked-up thinking, in the form of intrusive thoughts, anxious rumination, obsessions, and the voice of deep, dark depression, is the gift of a lifetime. I mention this short list of examples only because they are the specific kinds of mental projections that I have personally experienced. There are two primary reasons that I say this kind of thinking is a gift. Let's talk about those now.

If you have categorized yourself as someone who deals with a mental disorder, there is no question that you have learned over the course of your life to believe your thought life to be highly significant. In fact, you believe that your thoughts are so significant that certain ones are dangerous and worthy of fear. It has to be that way. If you didn't care about your thoughts, you would never take the time to label any of them as a problem or take on some sort of disorder label related to them.

So then, what method does life have to show you that you don't need to be afraid of your thoughts and emotions? Friends and therapists can tell you that your thoughts don't matter until they are blue in the face, and it most likely won't make the slightest difference because there is no way for you to be convinced that they really know what they are talking about. Not only that, but your mind will always come up with some sort of deeply convincing argument as to why those well-meaning people are wrong. The only effective way for life to show you that your thoughts and emotions mean nothing about your identity and abilities is to give you all of the thoughts and feelings that you believe you shouldn't have, so that you can see that they really, truly don't matter. They can grab your attention and send indescribable sensations through your body. But at the end of the day, they are inconsequential. They come, they put on their fireworks show and cause all sorts of suffering, and then they leave. They do this over and over again. Now, you can call this phenomenon a psychological disorder, or you can see it as life sending you a crystal clear message that, really, truly, your thoughts have nothing to do with you or reality. They have no power. They cause no action. They are stories and figments of a programmed imagination. They are meaningless in the sense that they carry not a bit of significance in relation to who we are or what we are capable of. At the same time, they are sweet messengers from the gods regarding the confusion and lies that we believe deep in our subconscious programming. Let's go back to the words of Carl Jung: "Until you make the unconscious conscious, it will direct your life and you will call it fate."

The dark, negative, sad, scary, destructive, anxious, nihilistic, and misanthropic thoughts and images that occupy your mind are the archangels sent to make your unconscious conscious. They are dramatic, gripping projections of an underlying belief of, "I am flawed and unsupported in the world." Please do not misinterpret what I am saying as "If you don't figure out your specific subconscious beliefs, then your worst nightmare will come true." That is not what I mean at all, and years ago, my own mind would have misconstrued it that way. What I mean is if you do not become conscious of a general belief of personal inadequacy and peril, and that this sort of belief is always inaccurate, then your peace and potential in this life will be unnecessarily limited.

Sadly, most people in our culture miss the lifeline that "mental illness" holds and go the route of adding complication to their lives by taking ownership of a new psychological disorder. I'm talking about the people who believe that their "mental illness" is simply a part of who they are and then proceed to either medicate it away or take up a lifelong crusade of trying to cure it (aka get rid of the bothersome symptoms). Our tendency to accept this diagnosed disorder narrative (instead of seeing fucked-up thinking as a gift) stems from our culture's misunderstanding of health and healing in general. We live in a society that is obsessed with suppressing any sort of suffering and doing anything to maintain a state of ease and comfort. This is clearly apparent if you are exposed to any form of modern-day advertising. The core message is always "If you buy this product, then your life will be easier and more comfortable." Companies use that messaging because it is what people crave.

Picture someone who eats fast food and doughnuts all the time and then just pounds antacids because they have "problems with indigestion." Picture someone who gets sick all the time and has a direct line to their prescription-happy physician who calls in yet another antibiotic and round of prednisolone at the pharmacy because they have a "problem with a weak immune system." Instead of seeing the heartburn as a guide of what not to eat and the frequent illness as an indication that maybe more nutrients and exercise would be helpful, the person clings to a "problem" and tries to make the discomfort go away.

This is exactly what we do with fucked-up thinking. The system is trying to show a discrepancy with reality in the belief structure or a misalignment. But instead of having the wisdom to be with the discomfort and see what the system is trying to show, we label ourselves with a "problem" and go to work running from the discomfort and doing anything to try to make the problem go away. This is such a waste! But it is also an easy misunderstanding to fix once we see what's going on. In fact, once you do begin to see what's going on, you can't help but start to shift—even if the shift is slow because our muscles are weak from a lifetime of avoidance.

Our systems are incredibly intelligent. They are always trying to auto-correct, to get back to health and wholeness. Suppression of symptoms really never makes sense. Just like heartburn has the ability to help someone see that they need to eat higher quality or healthier food and frequent illness can help someone see that they need to take better care of their body, fucked-up thinking can help someone see that they are holding onto untrue beliefs and have put all of their trust and hope into a fabricated version of themselves that only appears to exist in the mind.

Let me explain it this way. The other night, my daughter woke up in the middle of the night. I climbed into bed with her because she didn't want to be alone. She was wearing her new long-sleeved pajamas that have pictures of milk and cookies all over them because she couldn't wait to try them out, even though the weather was still quite hot. About an hour after I had gotten into bed with her, she had a nightmare and woke up again. When she woke up, she was quite upset because of the nightmare. She was also sweating and immediately said she badly needed to use the bathroom. After we got some cooler pajamas and she used the bathroom, she was still quite upset about the bad dream. I explained to her that the nightmare was her body's way of waking her up because she was too hot and needed to use the bathroom.

You might be wondering what this nightmare situation has to do with you. The answer is everything. The nightmare that you live in is trying to do the same for you. It's trying to wake you up from the miserable misunderstanding and confusion that you were taught to live by as a child. The voice that you have been so convinced is your voice and is calling the shots is trying to show you that it isn't. It isn't you, and it isn't calling the shots. Moreover, some of the core beliefs of inadequacy and lostness that are driving your behavior under the surface are completely untrue. What other method does the mind have to show you these things? If it whispered sweet nothings and beautiful stories in your mind, you would be mesmerized by it forever. No, it must go batshit crazy. You have to lose your mind so you can find yourself and what is true. It is the greatest move of true self-preservation imaginable.

Actually, let's look at the term "losing your mind" for just a minute. It's one of my favorites because it was one of my biggest fears for a long time. When people fear "losing their mind," they are usually referring to the fear of going insane. The modern-day diagnosis for this state would be psychosis, which can happen for periods with different mental disorders. However, the fear of going insane or losing one's mind usually refers to a schizophrenia spectrum disorder. People who are diagnosed with these kinds of disorders are often said to have "lost their mind." It's worth mentioning as a sidenote that this choice of words is wildly inappropriate. People who are dealing with psychosis have not lost their minds at all. In fact, a more accurate way to describe their situation is that they got lost IN their mind, causing them to detach from reality. The more someone bows out of real-life activities and responsibilities and turns their attention over to their mental landscape, the easier it is to get lost in the imagination.

My anxious mind and intrusive thought mechanisms had a complete heyday with this topic. I used to be in mid-conversation with a friend, and vivid thoughts of me turning into some sort of rabid dog sort of human who was aggressively running around, waving my head and salivating, would flash across my awareness. I would envision myself biting people, hurting little babies that I was carrying, or even violently headbutting the poor person I was talking to.

Whenever these topics come up that seem to be "hot buttons" for a particular mind, it's always an opportunity to appreciate the brilliance of the imagination. You might fear losing your job and ending up penniless, living under a bridge. You might fear dying alone to such an extent that nobody finds your body for weeks or even months. You might fear the judgment of others and imagine that acquaintances talk about you and laugh about you for hours after any social contact. You might (like I once did) fear that you are insufficient to hold the love and attention of your partner and catastrophize that he/she is more attracted to any person that possesses the qualities you feel you lack. The mind can produce stories and images that are so vivid and terrifying, and at the same time so incredibly disconnected from reality. I can remember a conversation that I had one time with some sort of holistic health therapist that I was working with to try to help with all of my anxiety and intrusive thought issues. She said something to me one time that I will never forget. I was tearfully and ashamedly admitting to her some of my intrusive thoughts—one of which was going "insane" and biting people. I think I said something like, "Sometimes when I'm talking to you, a thought pops into my head of me biting you." Without missing a beat, she responded, "Well, I'd just bite you back!"

I don't know if she was doing it intentionally, but with this simple statement, she was reminding me not of reality (nobody was bitten that day) but of how cause and effect work, how interaction happens in reality. You see, in the fearful images of my mind, the spotlight was completely on the wild, imaginary perils of the imaginary me. It's like watching a drama about the future, but staring at a stage that only has space for you. Nobody else exists. Other people's involvement and reactions are completely forgotten.

It is the movie of the wounded and broken child version of yourself. It has no end, and there is no hope of salvation. It is a film on replay with endless variations that will continue to carry meaning until it is seen for what it is, the movie of "I am broken and not enough."

However, the reality is that your body is being lived by intelligence, as are all the other bodies around you, and if you bite someone, the movie doesn't just stay focused on you and your demise. Nah, there will always be someone to bite you back.

If you can momentarily step back from the identification with the voice in your mind that says, "I hate this fear and I am so afraid of these thoughts!" and just acknowledge the sheer creativity of it, you can begin to appreciate it and even find it kind of funny. Your mind and my mind have endless ways of imagining the deep fears of inadequacy that we carry.

Honestly, it's merciful that they do, because these beliefs are so counter to what is true, so anti-reality that the mind must put them in front of our awareness so that we can see them and let go of them. If we don't become aware of them, they simply remain as a film across our awareness that silently colors and distorts our worldview. But when beliefs are given form in imaginary thoughts that grab our attention and cause intense reactions in our nervous system, we can see and experience the faulty beliefs that paralyze us and understand that they simply do not fit in reality. My fear of losing my mind and hurting people is a beautifully creative image to illustrate a deep and amorphous fear of being broken, evil, and wrong, and being a victim of an angry and unsupportive

God. Without these wild images, the beliefs were just operating under the surface, distorting my perceptions and my behavior. But the wild thoughts and fears are the gifts of the mind. Those are the mind saying, "Look! This is what you believe! This is trapped in your subconscious, and it's making your life so much harder than it needs to be! This is what you were taught, but if you look at reality for just a moment, you can see that it isn't true, and you don't have to believe it anymore! You can be free!"

Your fucked-up mind is trying to set you free.

And don't you forget it.

Let's return to the misnomer "lose your mind" for a moment. It tells us so much about our misunderstandings of mental health as a culture! We have fallen into the trap of believing that having a nice, neat, cleaned-up mind or imagination means being mentally healthy. In reality, a nice, neat, cleaned-up mind is equivalent to very low creativity. True mental health is a reflection of being highly differentiated from the mind (which comes with practice) and highly connected to the awareness that we are and the intelligence that moves our whole world. True mental health is having the confidence to watch the imagination wander to any imaginable high or low, knowing full well that the wandering only matters from a creative point of view. Hell, the best artists in the world have really fucked-up minds. It's basically a requirement.

How else would they come up with the art to captivate us? Think of artists like Francisco Goya and Salvador Dalí who had the audacity to depict disturbing images from their imaginations for public consumption. Think of Taylor Swift's award-winning song "Anti-Hero." These artists capture some of the potential highs and lows of the human psyche through creative imagery. We (the consumers) of their art can't get enough of it because it reflects real, raw emotion that we can connect to. Truly, health has nothing to do with the content of your mind and everything to do with identity—who you know or believe yourself to be.

PART 8
WAKING UP

CHAPTER 28
BUILD THE MUSCLE OF BEING WITH DISCOMFORT

The longer that I experience living in this body and study this topic of fucked-up-mindedness, the more I am convinced that there is one thing that makes the difference between flailing and fulfillment. That one thing is the ability to be with discomfort. People say that love makes the world go round. I do believe that is true because we are all love at the core. However, because of our deep state of confusion as a culture, I think it would be more accurate to say that what makes the world go round is the avoidance of discomfort.

We are all on the run all the time from the monster of discomfort. We ingest substances, we seek out relationships, we get jobs and degrees, and we buy tons and tons of shit all in an attempt to escape feelings of discomfort. And you know the other thing that we do to escape discomfort and find a good feeling? We think. And in the frenzied, ongoing thinking, we create an entire world based on fears, confusion, and misunderstanding. Each of us lives in our own version of that world. It is a world of endless exhaustion and unsolvable problems, and the protagonist, the mental image of ourselves that we believe ourselves to be, can never find real safety or relief because it is made of all the confusion and lies. So how do we exit this maze of the fucked-up mind? Is there any hope?

There is hope. There is an exit. It is through discomfort in the present moment. When we stop running to the mind and we stay with discomfort, we can exit the vortex and find ourselves on the solid ground of reality. And you know what? The discomfort passes. The burning, the tingling, the racing heart, the pressure. It passes. So does the mental shit that is desperately trying to grab your attention. It all passes. And what's left? This beating heart. This miraculous breathing. Problems. Solutions. Life engaging with life. Magic. Then we can start to see the marvel of existence that has always been there. We were only blind to it because we were captivated by a mind pretending to be me (and you).

People will often ask, "Ok, all of this is great, but how do I get better?" My response is this: The first step in getting better is realizing there was never a real problem in the first place. There was only confusion about your true identity and then a lot of imagined problems that seemed believable. Once you see this, your reality starts to recalibrate. The mind's stories get less interesting, less believable. Things that previously looked like unsolvable problems fizzle into thin air because they were never real problems to begin with. Then you start having far more energy and capacity to do things in real life because dealing with your mind is no longer a part-time (or even full-time) job. From there, the possibilities are endless depending on the person. And most likely, you'll still get caught up in mind-created problems and confusion sometimes. That's just part of being human. But those incidents become fewer and farther between as you practice living in the company of the mind with the wisdom that it has nothing to do with you.

CHAPTER 29
LOVE YOUR FUCKED-UP MIND

Don't hate your fucked-up mind (even though there is a voice in your mind that says that you do). Hold your fucked-up mind. Love your fucked-up mind. Be with your fucked-up mind. It went to work long ago, building a mental protagonist that could be your champion and help you to survive. Now that you are an adult, the same clever little mechanism is trying to help you once again by giving concept and form to the faulty beliefs that act as viruses within your system. If you stop running from dark, anxious, and crazy thoughts, they will heal you. They show you the confusion that you learned and how contrary it is to reality, to what is true.

And this is important, too. Don't try to make a science out of this. Don't be too prescriptive. Don't give all your dark and anxious thoughts laser attention, trying to identify all the different faulty beliefs and find a way to unravel and disprove each one. It's better to let the process be about sense and feeling. Get a sense of the pain that was inflicted on you as a child. Let yourself feel the lostness, the confusion, the belief in being wrong or broken, the terror of believing that the world or God is out to get you, and that you are unsupported in this life. Feel that while you are simultaneously lived by intelligence in this moment. Notice that you are breathed. You are moved. Even the most intricate motions of your fingers and the inner workings of your internal organs are done for you.

This noticing unwinds the confusion. It unravels the faulty beliefs. It dislodges the pain and deep-seated confusion. And before you know it, everything starts to shift. And I don't mean that all of your fears and insecurities fall away overnight and you get to have a neat, cleaned-up, happy mind, happily ever after. No. This is the work of a lifetime, and that kind of mind isn't the goal anyway.

The journey of being human is one of getting lost and then finding our way back home, creating a meaningful story in the process. And the mind is with us the whole way. The mind creates a protagonist from the confusion we inherit. The mind haunts us and gives us a reason to seek truth. The mind reveals what has been hidden and is causing pain under the surface. By doing this, the mind cracks open a passage way leading back to reality and what is true. Its disruption causes a crack in our perception of ourselves and reality, and that becomes our doorway to come home.

CHAPTER 30
THE MIND SAVES YOU, BUT NOT HOW YOU THINK

We are finally in a position to see that our bodies are being lived by intelligence (not by the mind) and that we are the awareness that perceives and listens to the mind. In noticing these things, we are invited to break the greatest addiction of all time: the addiction to the misuse of the imagination.

You believed that you were the voice speaking in first person in your mind, and so you've given that voice all your attention for as long as you can remember. You check in with it first thing in the morning. You consult it with every single problem or challenge. You respond to its criticisms and cruel remarks by meekly bowing your head and stopping everything else to listen. You wait for it to shift gears and say something positive and uplifting before starting back in motion. You repeatedly take your attention away from real life to give it your attention and a listening ear. Why do you and I do this? We do it because we believe that the voice is us, the greatest advocate for our lives. Before we know it, we can't stop. Our attention is continuously darting back to the blabbering mind. However, the mind was never meant to be a personal narrator. It is an imagination, designed to assist us with visualizing solutions to problems that we face *in reality*. Do you see the difference? Let me say it again. Your imagination was never meant to be used as a personal narrator. Doing so is a misguided coping mechanism resulting from trauma and misunderstanding.

But in a genius act of self-preservation, the mind, with its "I" voice, begins to go against what we believe and love. And we have the opportunity, once and for all, to see what it is and what we are.

In this way, the mind opens the door to freedom. But watch out, because as you see these things, the mind will start to talk about what you are seeing. It will take on the voice of the wise guru who once again sounds like your savior. It might also scold you for doing the healing process "wrong"—for not being mindful enough or for giving too much attention to its ramblings. The mind will never, ever save you through the content of its thoughts. It can only save you by showing you that you are not it, whereby giving you the strength to give up your dependence, your blind hypnosis to its monologues.

You will never be free as long as you are trying to have

the "right" thoughts and feelings. You are free when you see that you are big enough and great enough to hold every thought and emotion.

So give that fucked-up mind some of the loving attention and appreciation it deserves. Whatever it says doesn't matter. It has broken the spell of your mistaken identity. Let its craziness shatter your misconceptions and misunderstandings. And don't then expect or hope that it will become nice and clean again. Instead, give your attention back to reality. Watch how you are lived by intelligence. Then, seeing normal everyday life becomes the continuous experience of inexplicable magic. You might be sipping a cup of coffee and notice how your fingers expertly grip the handle of the mug so that it sits stably in your hand and how the gorgeous steam wafts out of the cup as if you are holding some ethereal magic potion. You might be engaging in normal discourse with colleagues at work and marvel at how the conversation bounces back and forth with different themes, how facial expressions change, how laughter erupts, and how decisions are made even though no individual mind is responsible for any of it. You might even take a moment now and then to sit in sheer astonishment at how you are living, breathing, and doing in a world of billions of other people, and not a single one of us can explain with utter certainty how or why we are here. The intelligence in you will start to notice these things (not the mind). I can remember when I first started studying these topics, I could feel that they were true, but I kept frantically looking to my mind to understand them and agree with them. I craved so much for my mind to "get it." And of course, my mind readily talked about trying to do so. It took some time for me to truly accept that my mind would never be capable of getting there. I had to fall out of love with my mind and fall in love with my inner wisdom and instinct for a time before I could let go of that futile pursuit. Taking attention away from the mind can feel a little bit like hurling yourself into thin air from the top of a tall building, but the reality is that you are held by the greatest love and care imaginable. And every moment that you are brave enough to do this, your alignment with life and truth grows stronger.

As the haze of the talking mind starts to subside, or at least captivate your attention less, you will also be surprised at how you see people and situations in a completely new light. I have seen this repeatedly with my children. One of my daughters is currently three years old. I think she is brilliant, but she also tends to be a bit long-winded, a bit short-tempered, and a bit particular about a lot of things. It's so easy to look at her through the haze of my mind's judgments. This looks like seeing her through a film of commentary, such as, "She's probably about to throw another fit," "I can't believe she is screaming again," "She'd better hurry up and wash her hands and stop playing with the damn water," etc. However, when I am conscious enough to look at her and to simply see what is actually there, I am speechless in amazement. I stare at this gorgeous little creature who is pulsating with so much energy that she is constantly flitting and fluttering—even when attempting to stand in place. Her eyes sparkle. Her wavy, loose curls bounce ever so slightly when she talks. Her cheeks are rosy and round, resembling a beautiful doll. She is pure magic incarnate. We all are. I am so thankful for the privilege to see her and the rest of my life in this way, even if it is for short intervals. It is new for me, and it is breathtaking.

The next chapter introduces some simple moment-to-moment practices that have helped me on my journey. But before we move on, I wanted to ask a small favor. If you have found this book helpful or meaningful, would you take one or two minutes to leave a review on Amazon? There are so many people who feel trapped in prisons created by their imaginations. You leaving a review will help this book to reach those people so that they don't have to stay in needless suffering. I would also love to hear your thoughts and experience. I've poured my heart into this book, and nothing is more encouraging or satisfying than knowing that my story and work made someone else's life better.

With so much love,
Katherine

CHAPTER 31
PRACTICES TO PROMOTE FREEDOM

I'm not a big fan of tools and techniques, but two present-moment shifts or practices have helped me in this journey of waking up to what is real and aligning with what is true. The first I will call the "Drop Down Method," and the second, I will call the "Rigorous Release Method."

The Drop Down Method

When I'm lost in my mind's commentary on reality (instead of actually being in reality), it feels like I'm in a cloudy haze hovering right above what is really happening. Let's say that I'm with my kids, and my mind starts criticizing my parenting. Maybe one of my daughters asks me to play, and I turn her down because I need to place a grocery order, or even because I just don't want to. The mind starts hurling accusations: "You don't play with them enough! You're always on your phone! You're not a fun mom! You've probably already damaged your bond with them because you don't give them enough individual attention." Along with these thoughts, the heat starts to rise in my body, and my face starts to burn a little while my jaw and shoulders tighten. The minute I notice that I'm lost in the mind's commentary and problems, I take it as a cue to drop down. I let go of the mind's commentary, criticism, and panicked monologue. I let go of it mid-sentence—without resolution, no need for rebuttals or logical disproving. It might not stop talking, but my attention starts to wane. I drop down, down from the haze of judgments and fears and scheming—down from the clouds and into this precious, magical moment. I look around the room. Two of my daughters are engrossed in a game of pretend. The daughter who asked me to play is diligently building an intricate tower out of magnetic tiles. My youngest pushes on my knee, begging me to read a book. Her eyes blink, and her eyelashes flutter. I still feel a little burning in my face, but I know it is not anything to worry about, just the old fear of not being enough. Magic is happening. I'm so thankful I now know to drop out of the thinking and pay attention to what is happening in the present, because the magic of this moment is precious, and the next moment isn't a guarantee. Drop down.

The Rigorous Release Method

Now let's talk rigorous release. Let's say my husband, children, and I have decided to go to Sunday brunch. My husband is driving and I am in the passenger's seat. I might have an intrusive thought about grabbing the steering wheel and driving off the road. Or a fearful thought of "What if someone runs into us while we are on this busy highway and seriously injures my two oldest daughters, who are sitting in the back seat?" The feeling of panic, hot, stifling, pulsating, and paralyzing, sets into my limbs. The tightness and tension in my legs, shoulders, and arms could strangle a hamster. The minute I notice this, I release the tension. I deeply exhale (usually I'm holding my breath in these moments) and I let my arms, legs, neck, and shoulders melt so that everything is hanging as loosely as possible.

I included the term "rigorous" in the title of this release method because it takes some determination. The mind won't tell you to do it; if anything, it will be screaming that you shouldn't because it isn't "safe." But you trust life enough to release, let go, and surrender anyway. By doing so, you grow your trust in and connection to the wisdom, intelligence, and love that you are, AND you allow the fear that rose up from your subconscious to flow out of you and be free instead of clinging to it as if doing so keeps you safe. Believe me, it doesn't.

It is also important to note that these shifts will start to happen automatically when you begin to truly see who you are and the irrelevance of your thoughts. When you first start learning these truths, it can be easy to get stuck in a cycle of listening to your mind try to force "mindfulness" on you and then get angry and frustrated at you when you "fail." This is just more mental gibberish and another imaginative projection of the deep fear of inadequacy. These shifts will never happen because of the mind saying they should. They happen automatically when they make sense to the intelligence of your being.

CONCLUSION

Our fucked-up minds have gotten such a bad rap. They've been demonized for so long. It's time to recognize their beauty and the key to freedom that they offer. There is no greater emancipation than being liberated from slavery to the mind. When a mind pretending to be me is finally seen for what it is, the tight limitations of the mental world and the "personality" are seen for the flimsy and immaterial clouds that they are.

Our mental disorders are not concrete viruses or bacteria or chemical discrepancies, but clever nightmares trying to awaken us. To recognize who you are and to differentiate from the mind is freedom from our conditioning—from our trauma and misguided training. This is the way home. We are vessels of pure intelligence, constantly learning, adapting, and enduring so that life can continue and flourish. Our potential is limitless. Our worth is beyond measure. We are made of inexplicable magic. And to think that we might never have known this if it weren't for a fucked-up mind.

A Mind Pretending to Be Me

REFERENCE LIST

Amoeba. (n.d.). *Britannica Kids*. Encyclopædia Britannica, Inc. Retrieved [August 6, 2025] from https://kids.britannica.com/students/article/amoeba/272840

Johnson, A. (2022, December 26). How you're living in the past and not realizing it (special rebroadcast), (232) [Audio podcast]. In *Changeable*. https://dramyjohnson.com/2022/12/ep232/

Maté, G. (2022, December 11). *Authenticity can heal trauma*. Mad in America; Science, Psychiatry and Social Justice. (How to Academy). https://www.madinamerica.com/2022/12/authenticity-can-heal-trauma-dr-gabor-mate-md/

Maté, G. & Maté, D. (2022). *The myth of normal: Trauma, illness, & healing in a toxic culture*. Avery, an imprint of Penguin House.

Mughal, F., Chew-Graham, C. A., Babatunde, O. O., Saunders, B., Meki, A., & Dikomitis, L. (2023). The functions of self-harm in young people and their perspectives about future general practitioner-led care: A qualitative study. *Health expectations: an international journal of public participation in health care and health policy, 26*(3), 1180–1188.
https://doi.org/10.1111/hex.13733

Neill, M. (2019, July 8). A Simpler Way of Being in The World, In *Blog*.
https://www.michaelneill.org/cfts1194/

Vygotsky, L. S. (1962). *Thought and language*. (E. Hanfmann & G. Vakar, Eds.). MIT Press.

www.ingramcontent.com/pod-product-compliance
Lightning Source LLC
LaVergne TN
LVHW010200070526
838199LV00062B/4431